Joint Workshop on Unsupervised and Semi-Supervised Learning in NLP 2012

(ROBUS-UNSUP 2012)

Held at the 13th Conference of the European Chapter of the Association for Computational Linguistics (EACL 2012)

Avignon, France
23 – 27 April 2012

ISBN: 978-1-62276-490-7

Printed from e-media with permission by:

Curran Associates, Inc.
57 Morehouse Lane
Red Hook, NY 12571

Some format issues inherent in the e-media version may also appear in this print version.

Printed by Curran Associates, Inc. (2012)

For permission requests, please contact the Association for Computational Linguistics at the address below.

Association for Computational Linguistics
209 N. Eighth Street
Stroudsburg, Pennsylvania 18360

Phone: 1-570-476-8006
Fax: 1-570-476-0860

acl@aclweb.org

Additional copies of this publication are available from:

Curran Associates, Inc.
57 Morehouse Lane
Red Hook, NY 12571 USA
Phone: 845-758-0400
Fax: 845-758-2634
Email: curran@proceedings.com
Web: www.proceedings.com

Foreword

In recent years, there has been an increased interest in minimizing the need for annotated data in NLP. Significant progress has been made in the development of both semi-supervised and unsupervised learning approaches. Semi-supervised approaches are already showing remarkable empirical success, with models that exploit mixtures of labeled and unlabeled data obtaining best results in several tasks. Although unsupervised approaches have proved more challenging than semi-supervised ones, their further development is particularly important because they carry the highest potential in terms of avoiding the annotation cost. Such approaches can be applied to any language or genre for which adequate raw text resources are available.

This workshop aimed to bring together researchers dedicated to designing and evaluating unsupervised and semi-supervised learning algorithms for NLP problems. The workshop accepted submissions in any topic related to unsupervised and semi-supervised learning. However, specific focus was given to two special themes: robust algorithms and explorations of the continuum from unsupervised to semi-supervised learning.

Robust Algorithms: By more robust unsupervised or semi-supervised learning algorithms we mean algorithms with few parameters that give good results across different data sets and/or different applications. Many algorithms including EM, self-training and co-training are very parameter-sensitive, and parameter tuning has therefore become an important research topic. We explicitly encourage submissions that present robust algorithms or evaluate the robustness of known algorithms.

The Continuum from Unsupervised to Semi-Supervised Learning: The distinction between unsupervised and semi-supervised learning approaches is often not very clear, and we explicitly encourage submissions about grey-zone approaches such as weak and indirect supervision, learning from nearly free annotations (e.g. html mark-up), joint learning from several modalities, cross-language adaptation, and learning with knowledge-based priors or posteriors.

The workshop was carried out as a joint workshop between two workshop series. Predecessors are UNSUP-2011 — First Workshop on Unsupervised Learning in NLP (held at EMNLP 2011, Edinburgh, Scotland, UK) and ROBUS 2011 - Workshop on Robust Unsupervised and Semisupervised Methods in Natural Language Processing (in conjunction with RANL 2011, Hissar, Bulgaria). We invited technical papers as well as survey and position papers.

For the workshop, we received 10 submissions, of which we accepted 7.

Avignon, April 2012

The organizing committee

Organizers:

Omri Abend (Hebrew University of Jerusalem)
Chris Biemann (TU Darmstadt)
Anna Korhonen (University of Cambridge)
Ari Rappoport (Hebrew University of Jerusalem)
Roi Reichart (MIT)
Anders Søgaard (University of Copenhagen)

Program Committee:

Steven Abney (University of Michigan, USA)
Jason Baldridge (University of Texas at Austin, USA)
Phil Blunsom (Oxford University, UK)
Stefan Bordag (ExB Research & Development)
Sam Brody (Rutgers University, USA)
Alexander Clark (Royal Holloway, University of London, UK)
Shay Cohen (Columbia University, USA)
Trevor Cohn (University of Sheffield, UK)
Gregory Druck (University of Massachusetts Amherst, USA)
Eugenie Giesbrecht (FZI Karlsruhe)
Joao Graca (University of Pennsylvania, USA)
Florian Holz (University of Leipzig)
Jonas Kuhn (University of Stuttgart)
Percy Liang (University of Stanford, USA)
Suresh Manandhar (University of York, UK)
Diana McCarthy (Lexical Computing, Ltd., UK)
Preslav Nakov (Qatar Computing Research Institute, Qatar Foundation)
Roberto Navigli (University of Rome, Italy)
Vincent Ng (UT Dallas, USA)
Andreas Vlachos (University of Cambridge, UK)
Reinhard Rapp (JG University of Mainz)
Andrew Rosenberg (CUNY, USA)
Sabine Schulte im Walde (University of Stuttgart, Germany)
Noah A. Smith (CMU, USA)
Valentin I. Spitkovsky (University of Stanford, USA)
Torsten Zesch (TU Darmstadt)

Table of Contents

Conference Program

Fast Unsupervised Dependency Parsing with Arc-Standard Transitions
Mohammad Sadegh Rasooli and Heshaam Faili

Dependency-Based Open Information Extraction
Pablo Gamallo, Marcos Garcia and Santiago Fernández-Lanza

Sweeping through the Topic Space: Bad luck? Roll again!
Martin Riedl and Chris Biemann

Clustered Word Classes for Preordering in Statistical Machine Translation
Sara Stymne

Improving Distantly Supervised Extraction of Drug-Drug and Protein-Protein Interactions
Tamara Bobic, Roman Klinger, Philippe Thomas and Martin Hofmann-Apitius

Robust Induction of Parts-of-Speech in Child-Directed Language by Co-Clustering of Words and Contexts
Richard E Leibbrandt and David MW Powers

Dependency Parsing Domain Adaptation using Transductive SVM
Antonio Valerio Miceli Barone and Giuseppe Attardi

Fast Unsupervised Dependency Parsing with Arc-Standard Transitions

Mohammad Sadegh Rasooli
Department of Computer Engineering
Iran University of Science and Technology
Narmak, Tehran, Iran
rasooli@comp.iust.ac.ir
rasooli.ms@gmail.com

Heshaam Faili
School of Electrical
and Computer Engineering
University of Tehran
Amir-Abaad, Tehran, Iran
hfaili@ut.ac.ir

Abstract

Unsupervised dependency parsing is one of the most challenging tasks in natural languages processing. The task involves finding the best possible dependency trees from raw sentences without getting any aid from annotated data. In this paper, we illustrate that by applying a supervised incremental parsing model to unsupervised parsing; parsing with a linear time complexity will be faster than the other methods. With only 15 training iterations with linear time complexity, we gain results comparable to those of other state of the art methods. By employing two simple universal linguistic rules inspired from the classical dependency grammar, we improve the results in some languages and get the state of the art results. We also test our model on a part of the ongoing Persian dependency treebank. This work is the first work done on the Persian language.

1 Introduction

Unsupervised learning of grammars has achieved considerable focus in recent years. The lack of sufficient manually tagged linguistic data and the considerable successes of unsupervised approaches on some languages have motivated researchers to test different models of unsupervised learning on different linguistic representations.

Since the introduction of the dependency model with valence (DMV) proposed by Klein and Manning (2004), dependency grammar induction has received great attention by researchers. DMV was the first model to outperform the right attachment accuracy in English. Since this achievement, the model has been used by many researchers (e.g. (Cohen and Smith, 2010); (Gillenwater et al., 2011); (Headden III et al., 2009); and (Spitkovsky et al., 2011b)).

The main task of unsupervised dependency parsing is to obtain the most likely dependency tree of a sentence without using any annotated training data. In dependency trees, each word has only one head and the head of the sentence is a dependent of an artificial root word. Problems such as data sparsity and a large search space that increases the ambiguity have made the task difficult. Even deciding the direction of the link between two words in a dependency relation has made the task more difficult than finding phrase structures themselves (Klein and Manning, 2004).

In this paper, we propose a model based on Arc-Standard Transition System of Nivre (2004), which is known as an incremental greedy projective parsing model that parses sentences in linear time. To the best of our knowledge, the only incremental unsupervised dependency parsing is the model of Daumé III (2009) with Shift-Reduce parsing model (Nivre, 2003).[1]

Our model is not lexicalized, has a simple feature space and converges in 15 iterations with a linear ($O(n)$) parsing and training time, while other methods based on DMV in the best case work in $O(n^3)$ time complexity with $O(n^3)$ memory use for sentences with of length n. We believe that the output of this model can also improve DMV.[2] In addition, we use punctuation clues (Spitkovsky et al., 2011c), tying feature similarity in the transition system configuration, and

[1]The other study is in Seginer (2007) that is for constituency parsing (phrase structure extraction).

[2]For the effect of model initialization in unsupervised dependency parsing, see Gimpel and Smith (2011).

"baby steps" notion (Spitkovsky et al., 2009) to improve the model accuracy.

We test our model on 9 CoNLL 2006 and 2007 shared task data sets (Buchholz and Marsi, 2006; Nivre et al., 2007) and WSJ part of Penn treebank and show that in some languages our model is better than the recent models. We also test our model on a part of an ongoing first Persian dependency corpus (Rasooli et al., 2011). Our study may be the first work to test dependency parsing on the Persian language.

The remainder of this paper is organized as follows. In Section 2, related work on unsupervised dependency parsing is reviewed. In Section 3, we describe our dependency parsing model. In Section 4 and Section 5, after the reporting experimental results on several languages, the conclusion is made.

2 Related Work

The first considerable work on unsupervised dependency parsing which outperforms the baseline (right attachment) accuracy in English was proposed by Klein and Manning (2004). The model is called dependency model with valence (DMV). In the DMV, each word can be the head of the sentence with the probability of $P(root|X)$. Each word X, decides to get a child Y from a direction (right or left), with the probability $P_{CHOOSE}(X|Y, dir, adj)$, where adj is a Boolean value indicating whether the word has gotten a child in the direction dir or not. The other probability used in the DMV is $P_{STOP}(X|Y, dir, adj)$ that means whether to stop getting dependents from the direction with adjacency value or not. All the probabilities in the model are assumed to be independent and the dependency tree likelihood is a product of all probabilities. Only part of speech (POS) tags are used as features and the probabilities are multinomial. The model uses the inside-outside algorithm to find all possible subtrees efficiently in Expectation Maximization (EM) algorithm.

Several researchers have tried to improve and modify the DMV. In Headden III et al. (2009), by using the lexical values with the frequency more than 100 and defining tied probabilistic context free grammar (PCFG) and Dirichlet priors, the accuracy is improved. In Smith and Eisner (2005), by producing artificial neighbors of the feature space via actions such as deletion of one word, substitution of adjacent words and adding a word, the likelihood of the true feature space in all neighbors is calculated. That method is known as contrastive estimation (CE).

In Spitkovsky et al. (2009), the idea of learning the initial parameters of the model from shorter sentences leads to a method named "baby steps". In "baby steps", the model prior of each training set with the sentence length less than or equal to N, is achieved by training DMV on the training set with the sentence length less than or equal to $N - 1$. The other method used in the mentioned work, is "less is more" which hypothesize that training on a subset of all data (with the length of less than or equal to 15) in batch mode is more useful than training on all data. In Spitkovsky et al. (2010a), a combination of "baby steps" and "less is more", named "leapfrog" is applied to the DMV. In Spitkovsky et al. (2011b), a mixture of EMs is used to improve the DMV by trying to escape from local maxima; i.e., changing the EM policy in some iterations in order to escape from local maxima. The model is termed "lateen" EM. In Spitkovsky et al. (2010b), HTML hypertext tags are used as indicators of phrases in order to localize the search space of the dependency model. In Spitkovsky et al. (2011c), punctuation marks are used as indicators of local dependencies of the words in the sentence.

In Cohen and Smith (2010), shared logistic normal distribution is used to tie grammatical roles that are not assumed to be independent from each other. In the study, the bilingual similarity of each POS tag probability in the dependency model is applied to the probability model. In Blunsom and Cohn (2010), Pitman-Yor priors (PYP) are applied to the DMV. Furthermore, tree substitution grammar (TSG) is used as an intermediate representation of the tree. In Gillenwater et al. (2011), a mathematical model is employed to overcome the posterior sparsity in the DMV, by defining constraints on the probability model.

There are also some models different from DMV. In Daumé III (2009), based on a stochastic search method, Shift-Reduce transition parsing model of Nivre (2003) is applied. The model is greedy and selects an action stochastically according to each action probability at the time. The advantage of the model lies on its parsing and training speed. In Naseem and Barzilay (2011), sparse semantic annotations in texts are used as

Initialization	$\langle nil, W, \Phi \rangle$
Termination	$\langle S, nil, A \rangle$
Left-Reduce	$\langle w_i w_j \vert S, I, A \rangle \rightarrow \langle w_j \vert S, I, A \cup \langle w_j, w_i \rangle \rangle$
Right-Reduce	$\langle w_i w_j \vert S, I, A \rangle \rightarrow \langle w_i \vert S, I, A \cup \langle w_i, w_j \rangle \rangle$
Shift	$\langle S, w_i \vert I, A \rangle \rightarrow \langle w_i \vert S, I, A \rangle$

Figure 1: Actions in Arc-Standard Transition System (Nivre, 2004)

clues to unsupervised parsing. In Mareček and Žabokrtský (2011), by applying Gibbs sampling method to count the data occurrences, a simple probability model (the fraction of each dependency relation divided by the number of head POS tags) is used. In that model, non-projective dependency trees are allowed and all noun-root dependency probabilities are multiplied by a small number, to decrease the chance of choosing a noun-root dependency. There are also some studies in which labeled data in one language is employed to guide unsupervised parsing in the others (Cohen et al., 2011).

3 Fast Unsupervised Parsing

In this section, after a brief description of the Arc-Standard parsing model, our probability model, and the unsupervised search-based structure prediction (Daumé III, 2009) are reviewed. After these descriptions, we go through "baby steps," the use of curricula in unsupervised learning (Tu and Honavar, 2011), and the use of punctuation in unsupervised parsing. Finally, we describe our tied feature model that tries to overcome the data sparsity. In this paper, a mixture of "baby steps" and punctuation clues along with search-based structure prediction is applied to the Arc-Standard model.

3.1 Arc-Standard Transition Model

The parser in this model has a configuration represented by $\langle S, I, A \rangle$, where S is a stack of words, I is a buffer of input words which are not processed yet and A is the list of all arcs that are made until now. The parser initializes with $\langle nil, W, \phi \rangle$ in which W is a string of all words in the sentence, nil shows a stack with a root word and Φ shows an empty set. The termination configuration is shown as $\langle S, nil, A \rangle$, where S shows an empty stack with only root word, nil shows an empty buffer and A is the full arc set. An arc in which w_j is the head of w_i is shown by $w_j \rightarrow w_i$ or (w_j, w_i).

As shown in Figure 1, there are three actions in this model. In the shift action, the top-most input word goes to the top of the stack. In the left-reduce action, the top-most stack word becomes the head of the second item in the stack and the second item is removed from the stack. On the other hand, in the right-reduce action, the second word in the stack becomes the head of the top item in the stack and the top item is removed from the stack.

3.2 Feature Space and Probability Model

The feature space that we use in this model is a tuple of three POS tags; i.e., the first item in the buffer, the top-most and the second item in the stack. The probability of each action is inspired from Chelba and Jelinek (2000) as in equation (1). In each step in the configuration, the parser chooses an action based on the probability in equation (1), where $feat$ is the feature value and act is an action.

$$P(act, feat) = P(act) \cdot P(feat|act) \qquad (1)$$

The action selection in the training phase is done stochastically. In other words, in every step there is a maximum of 3 actions and a minimum of one action.[3] After calculating all probabilities, a roulette wheel is made to do multinomial sampling. The sampling is done with stochastic EM (Celeux and Diebolt, 1985) in a roulette wheel selection model.

The probabilities are initialized equally (except that $P(shift) = 0.5$ and $P(right - reduce) = P(left - reduce) = 0.25$). After sampling from the data, we update the model as in equations 2–4, where σ is a smoothing variable and N_f is the number of all possible unique features in the data set. $C(\cdot)$ is a function that counts the data from

[3]For example, in the first state only shift is possible and in the last state only right-reduce is possible.

samples. In equations 3 and 4, sh, $r-r$ and $l-r$ are shift, right-arc and left-arc actions respectively. $C(Action, Feature)$ is obtained from the samples drawn in the training phase. For example, if the right-reduce action is selected, we add its probability to $C(right-reduce, feature)$.

$$P(feat|act) = \frac{C(act, feat) + \sigma}{C(act) + N_f \sigma} \quad (2)$$

$$P(sh) = 0.5 \quad (3)$$

$$P(act) = \frac{C(act) + \sigma}{C(r-r) + C(l-r) + 2\sigma}; \quad act \neq Shift \quad (4)$$

3.3 Unsupervised Search-Based Structure Prediction

Since there are 3^{2n+1} possible actions for a sentence with the length of n it seems impractical to track the search space for even middle-length sentences. Accordingly, in Daumé III (2009) a stochastic search model is designed to improve the model accuracy based on random actions. In that work, with each configuration step, the trainer selects one of the actions according to the probability of each action stochastically. By choosing actions stochastically, a set of samples is drawn from the data and the model parameters are updated based on the pseudo-code in Figure 2. In Figure 2, π is known as the policy of the probability model and β is a constant number which changes in each iteration based on the iteration number ($\beta = \frac{1}{iteration\#^3}$). We employ this model in our work to learn probability values in equation 1. The learning from samples is done via equations (2–4).

```
Initialize π = π*
while not converge
  Take samples stochastically
  h ← learn from samples
  π = βπ + (1 − β)h
end while
return π
```

Figure 2: Pseudo-code of the search-based structure prediction model in Daumé III (2009)

3.4 "Baby Steps" Incremental Parsing

In Spitkovsky et al (2009), the idea that shorter sentences are less ambiguous, hence more informative, is applied to the task. Spitkovsky et al. (2009) emphasize that starting from sentences with a length of 1 and iterating on sentences with the $length \leq N$ from the probabilities gained from the sentences with the $length \leq N-1$, leads to better results.

We also use "baby steps" on our incremental model. For the sentences having length 1 through 5, we only iterate once in each sentence length. At those sentence lengths, the full search space is explored (all trees are made by doing all possible actions in each state of all possible configurations), while for sentence length 6 towards 15, we iterate at each step 3 times, only choosing one action stochastically at each state. The procedure is done similarly for all languages with the same parameters. In fact, the greedy nature of the model encourages us to bail out of each sentence length quickly. In other words, we want to jump out of early local maxima, as in early-terminating lateen EM (Spitkovsky et al., 2011b).

In curricula (Tu and Honavar, 2011), smoothing variable for shorter sentences is larger than smoothing variable for longer sentences. With regards to the idea, we start with smoothing variable equal to 1 and multiply it on each sentence length by a constant value equal to e^{-1}.

3.5 Punctuation Clues

Spitkovsky et al. (2011c) show that about 74.0% of words in English texts occurring between two punctuation marks have only one word linking with other words of the sentence. This characteristic is known as "loose". We apply this restriction on our model to improve the parsing accuracy and decrease the total search space. We show that this clue not only does not improve the dependency parsing accuracy, but also decreases it in some occasions.

3.6 Tying Probabilities with Feature Similarity Measure

We assume that the most important features in the feature set for right-reduce and left-reduce actions are the two top words in the stack. On the other hand, for the shift action, the most important words are first buffer and top stack words. In order to solve the sparsity problem, we modify the probability of each action based on equation (5). In this equation, $neigh(act, feat)$ is gained via searching over all features with the same top and second stack item for left-reduce and right-reduce, and all features with the same top stack and first buffer item for the shift action.

$$P'(feat|act) = \frac{P(feat|act) + \frac{\sum_{f' \in neigh(act,feat)} P(f'|act)}{C(neigh(act,feat))}}{2} \quad (5)$$

3.7 Universal Linguistic Heuristics to Improve Parsing Accuracy

Based on the nature of dependency grammar, we apply two heuristics. In the first heuristic, we multiply the probability of the last verb reduction by 10^{-10} in order to keep verbocentricity of the dependency grammar. The last verb reduction occurs when there is neither a verb in the buffer nor in the stack except the one that is going to be reduced by one of the right-arc or left-arc actions. In other words, the last verb remaining on the stack should be less likely to be removed than the other actions in the current configuration.[4] In the second heuristic, in addition to the first heuristic, we multiply each $noun \rightarrow verb$, $adjective \rightarrow verb$, and $adjective \rightarrow noun$ by 0.1 in order to keep the nature of dependency grammar in which nouns and adjective in most cases are not able to be the head of a verb and an adjective is not able to be the head of a noun.[5] We show in the experiments that, in most languages, considering this nature will help improve the parsing accuracy.

We have tested our model on 9 CoNLL data sets (Buchholz and Marsi, 2006; Nivre et al., 2007). The data sets include Arabic, Czech, Bulgarian, Danish, Dutch, Portuguese, Slovenian, Spanish, and Swedish. We have also tested our model on a part of the ongoing project of Persian dependency treebank. The data set includes 2,113 train and 235 test sentences.[6]

As shown in Figure 3, we use the same procedure as in Daumé III (2009), except that we restrict β to not be less than 0.005 in order to increase the chance of finding new search spaces stochastically. As in previous works, e.g., Smith and Eisner (2005), punctuation is removed for evaluation.

```
iteration# = 0
for i=1 to 15 do
 Train-set=all sentences-length≤i
  max-iter=3
  if(i≤ 5)
    max-iter=1
  end-if
 for j=1 to max-iter do
   β = max(1/iteration#^3, 0.005)
   iteration# ← iteration# + 1
   if(i ≤ 5)
     samples← find all subtrees
    end-if
    else
     samples← sample instances stochastically
    end-else
  h ← learn from samples
  π = βπ + (1 − β)h
 end-for
 σ = σ × e^-1
end-for
```

Figure 3: Pseudo-code of the unsupervised Arc-Standard training model

4 Evaluation Results

Although training is done on sentences of length less than 16, the test was done on all sentences in the test data without dropping any sentences form the test data. Results are shown in Table 1 on 9 languages. In Table 1, "h1" and "h2" refer to the two linguistic heuristics that are used in this paper. We also compare our work with Spitkovsky et al. (2011b) and Mareček and Žabokrtský (2011)

[4]It is important to note that the only reason that we choose a very small number is to decrease the chance of verb-reduction among three possible actions. Using other values≤ 0.01 does not change results significantly.

[5]The are some exceptions too. For example, in the sentence: "I am certain your work is good." Because of that, we do not choose a very small number.

[6]This dataset is obtained via contacting with the project team at http://www.dadegan.ir/en/. Recently an official pre-version of the dataset is released, consisting more than 12,000 annotated sentences (Dadegan Research Group, 2012). We wish to report results on the dataset in our future publications.

	Baselines			Using Heuristic 1 and 2			Using Heuristic 1		Without any heuristic	
Language	**Rand**	**LA**	**RA**	**fs+punc**	**fs**	**punc**	**fs+punc**	**punc**	**punc+fs**	**simp.**
Arabic'07	3.90	**59.00**	06.00	52.05	52.05	52.05	54.55	54.55	**55.64**	**55.64**
Bulgarian	8.00	38.80	17.90	52.48	**53.86**	46.36	42.75	37.35	35.99	35.99
Czech'07	7.40	29.60	24.20	42.37	**42.40**	39.31	30.21	27.94	25.17	25.17
Danish	6.70	47.80	13.10	52.14	**53.11**	52.14	51.10	51.70	46.01	46.01
Dutch	7.50	24.50	28.00	48.14	**48.80**	48.20	28.30	28.36	23.47	23.45
Persian	9.50	03.90	29.16	**51.65**	51.37	50.99	49.78	50.99	26.87	26.87
Portuguese	5.80	31.20	25.80	54.86	**55.84**	46.82	33.84	33.62	28.83	28.83
Slovenian	7.90	**26.60**	24.30	**22.44**	**22.44**	22.43	21.31	21.30	19.47	19.45
Spanish	4.30	29.80	24.70	30.88	31.16	30.88	**32.33**	**32.33**	29.63	29.69
Swedish	7.80	27.80	25.90	32.74	**34.33**	33.52	28.48	28.48	25.74	25.74
Turkish	6.40	01.50	**65.40**	33.83	27.39	38.13	**61.27**	47.92	30.56	34.52
Average	6.84	29.14	25.86	**43.05**	42.98	41.89	39.45	37.69	31.58	31.94

Table 1: Results tested on CoNLL data sets and the Persian data set. "Rand", "LA" and "RA" stand for random, left-attach and right-attach, respectively; "punc" refers to punctuation clues and fs refers to feature similarity cue; "all" refers to using both heuristics h1 and h2; and "simp." refers to the simple model.

in Table 2. As shown in Table 2, our model outperforms the accuracy in 7 out of 9 languages.

The Effect of Feature Similarity

As shown in Table 1, feature similarity cannot have any effect on the simple model. When we add linguistic information to the model, this feature similarity measure keeps the trainer from diverging. In other words, the greedy nature of the model becomes endangered when incomplete knowledge (as in our linguistic heuristics) is used. Incomplete knowledge may cause early divergence. In other words, the greedy algorithm tracks the knowledge which it has and does not consider other probable search areas. This phenomenon may cause early divergence in the model. By using feature similarity, we try to escape from this event.

The Effect of Punctuation Clues

As shown in Table 1, in most languages punctuation clues do not improve the accuracy. This maybe arises out of the fact that "loose" is not a good clue for incremental parsing. The other clue is "sprawl" in which the external link restriction is lifted. This restriction is in 92.9% of fragments in English texts (Spitkovsky et al., 2011c), but it is not implemented and tested in this paper.

4.1 Evaluation on English

We also test our data on Penn Treebank but we do not gain better results than state of the art methods. We use the same train and test set as in Spitkovsky et al. (2009). We convert the Penn treebank data via automatic "head-percolation" rules (Collins, 1999). We have also tested our model via simple stochastic EM (without using unsupervised structure prediction) and show that the main problem with this method in English is its fast divergence when jumping from sentence length 5 to 6. In the model settings tested for English, the model with heuristic 1 with the feature similarity is the best setting that we find. By testing with a smoothing variable ten times bigger

Model	WSJ'10	$WSJ'\infty$
h1+fs	45.16	31.97
h1+fs+punc	44.17	30.17
Stoch. EM(1-5)	40.86	33.65
Stoch. EM(1-5)+h1	52.70	42.85
Stoch. EM(1-5)+h1+h2	50.30	41.37
A1+fs+h1	49.9	43.3
Klein and Manning (2004)	43.2	-
Daumé III (2009)	45.4	-
Blunsom and Cohn (2010)	67.7	55.7
Spitkovsky et al. (2011a)	-	**59.1**

Table 3: Results of our model on WSJ, compared to its counterpart Daumé III (2009) and other DMV-based models. Since in Blunsom and Cohn (2010) and Spitkovsky et al. (2011b), other results are reported, we only limit our report to some of the results on WSJ. In the Table, "h1" shows heuristic 1 and "fs" shows the use of feature similarity. Stochastic EM(1-5) is one test that have done only by applying baby steps on sentences with the length 1 to 5 without using unsupervised search-based model. A1 refers to a change in the model in which smoothing variable in steps 1 to 5 is multiplied by 10.

Language \ Method Name	MZ-NR	MZ	Spi5	Spi6	Our Best
Arabic'07	24.8	25.0	22.0	49.5	**55.64**
Bulgarian	51.4	25.4	44.3	43.9	**53.86**
Czech'07	33.3	24.3	31.4	28.4	**42.40**
Danish	38.6	30.2	44.0	38.3	**53.11**
Dutch	43.4	32.2	32.5	27.8	**48.80**
Persian	-	-	-	-	**51.65**
Portuguese	41.8	43.2	34.4	36.7	**55.84**
Slovenian	**34.6**	25.4	33.6	32.2	22.44
Spanish	**54.6**	53.0	33.3	50.6	32.33
Swedish	26.9	23.3	42.5	**50.0**	34.33
Turkish	32.1	32.2	33.4	35.9	**61.27**
Average (except Persian)	38.1	31.4	35.1	39.3	**46.00**

Table 2: Comparison of our work to those of Table 5 ("Spi5") and Table 6 ("Spi6") in Spitkovsky et al. (2011b) and Mareček and Žabokrtský (2011) with Noun-Root constraint ("MZ-NR") and no constraint ("MZ"). The comparison results are from Table 4 in Mareček and Žabokrtský (2011). "Our Best" refers to the bold scores in Table 1.

in the first 5 steps, we have seen that the results change significantly. The results are shown in Table 3.

One main problem of the converted dependencies in English is their conversion errors like multi-root trees.[7] There are many trees in the corpus that have wrong multi-root dependencies. Such problems lead us to believe that we should not rely too much on the results on WSJ part of the Penn treebank.

5 Analysis and Conclusion

One main aspect of incremental methods is their similarity to the way that humans read and learn sentences in language. The interesting characteristic of incremental parsing lies on its speed and low memory use. In this paper, we use one new incremental parsing model on unsupervised parsing for the first time. The simple mathematical model and its linear training order has made the model flexible to be used for bigger data sets. In addition to testing recently used heuristics in unsupervised parsing, by inspiring basic dependency theory from linguistics, parsing accuracy has been increased in some languages. We see that this model is capable of detecting many true dependencies in many languages.

Some observations show that choosing inappropriate parameters for the model may lead to unwanted divergence in the model. The divergence is mostly seen in English, where we see a significant accuracy decrease at the last step in comparison to step 5 instead of seeing an increase in the accuracy. With one setting in English, we reach the accuracy equal to 43% (13% more than the accuracy of the model reported in this paper).

In some languages like Slovenian, we see that even with a good undirected accuracy, the model does not succeed in finding the dependency direction with heuristics. While in Czech, Dutch, and Bulgarian the second heuristic works well, it does not change accuracy a lot in other languages (in languages like Turkish and English this heuristic decreases accuracy). We believe that choosing better linguistic knowledge like the ones in Naseem et al. (2010), tying grammatical rules from other languages similar to the work in Cohen and Smith (2010), and choosing better probability models that can be enriched with lexical features and broad context consideration (like the works in supervised incremental dependency parsing) will help the model perform better on different languages.

Despite the fact that our study is the first work done on Persian, we believe that the results that we achieve for Persian is very considerable, regarding the free-word order nature of the Persian language.

[7] We assume to find only trees that are projective and single-rooted.

Acknowledgments

The paper is funded by Computer Research Center of Islamic Sciences (CRCIS). We would like to appreciate Valentin Spitkovsky and Shay Cohen for their technical comments on the research and paper draft. We would also thank Maryam Faal-Hamedanchi, Manouchehr Kouhestani, Amirsaeid Moloodi, Hamid Reza Ghader, Maryam Aminian and anonymous reviewers for their comments on the draft version. We would also like to thank Jason Eisner, Mark Johnson, Noah Smith and Joakim Nivre for their help in answering our questions and Saleh Ziaeinejad and Younes Sangsefidi for their help on the project.

References

Phil Blunsom and Trevor Cohn. 2010. Unsupervised induction of tree substitution grammars for dependency parsing. In *2010 Conference on Empirical Methods in Natural Language Processing (EMNLP 2010)*, pages 1204–1213.

Sabine Buchholz and Erwin Marsi. 2006. CoNLL-X shared task on multilingual dependency parsing. In *Proceeding of the Tenth Conforence on Computational Natural Language Learning (CoNLL)*.

Gilles Celeux and Jean Diebolt. 1985. The SEM algorithm: A probabilistic teacher algorithm derived from the em algorithm for the mixture problem. *Computational Statistics Quarterly*, 2:73–82.

Ciprian Chelba and Frederick Jelinek. 2000. Structured language modeling. *Computer Speech & Language*, 14(4):283–332.

Shay B. Cohen and Noah A. Smith. 2010. Covariance in unsupervised learning of probabilistic grammars. *Journal of Machine Learning Research (JMLR)*, 11:3117–3151.

Shay B. Cohen, Dipanjan Das, and Noah A. Smith. 2011. Unsupervised structure prediction with Non-Parallel multilingual guidance. In *Conference on Empirical Methods in Natural Language Processing (EMNLP 2011)*.

Michael Collins. 1999. *Head-driven statistical models for natural language parsing*. Ph.D. thesis, University of Pennsylvania.

Dadegan Research Group. 2012. *Persian Dependency Treebank Version 0.1, Annotation Manual and User Guide*. `http://dadegan.ir/en/`.

Hal Daumé III, John Langford, and Daniel Marcu. 2009. Search-based structured prediction. *Machine Learning*, 75(3):297–325.

Hal Daumé III. 2009. Unsupervised search-based structured prediction. In *26th International Conference on Machine Learning (ICML)*, pages 209–216. ACM.

Jennifer Gillenwater, Kuzman Ganchev, João Graça, Fernando Pereira, and Ben Taskar. 2011. Posterior sparsity in unsupervised dependency parsing. *Journal of Machine Learning Research (JMLR)*, 12:455–490.

Kevin Gimpel and Noah A. Smith. 2011. Concavity and initialization for unsupervised dependency grammar induction. Technical report.

William P. Headden III, Mark Johnson, and David McClosky. 2009. Improving unsupervised dependency parsing with richer contexts and smoothing. In *Human Language Technologies: The 2009 Annual Conference of the North American Chapter of the ACL*, pages 101–109.

Dan Klein and Christopher D. Manning. 2004. Corpus-based induction of syntactic structure: Models of dependency and constituency. In *Association for Computational Linguistics (ACL)*.

David Mareček and Zdeněk Žabokrtský. 2011. Gibbs sampling with treeness constraint in unsupervised dependency parsing. In *RANLP Workshop on Robust Unsupervised and Semisupervised Methods in Natural Language Processing*.

Tahira Naseem and Regina Barzilay. 2011. Using semantic cues to learn syntax. In *25th Conference on Artificial Intelligence (AAAI-11)*.

Tahira Naseem, Harr Chen, Regina Barzilay, and Mark Johnson. 2010. Using universal linguistic knowledge to guide grammar induction. In *2010 Conference on Empirical Methods in Natural Language Processing (EMNLP 2010)*.

Joakim Nivre, Johan Hall, Sandra Kübler, Ryan McDonald, Jens Nilsson, Sebastian Riedel, and Deniz Yuret. 2007. The CoNLL 2007 shared task on dependency parsing. In *Proceeding of CoNLL 2007*.

Joakim Nivre. 2003. An efficient algorithm for projective dependency parsing. In *International Workshop on Parsing Technologies*, pages 149–160.

Joakim Nivre. 2004. Incrementality in deterministic dependency parsing. In *Workshop on Incremental Parsing: Bringing Engineering and Cognition Together*, pages 50–57.

Mohammad Sadegh Rasooli, Amirsaeid Moloodi, Manouchehr Kouhestani, and Behrouz Minaei-Bidgoli. 2011. A syntactic valency lexicon for Persian verbs: The first steps towards Persian dependency treebank. In *5th Language & Technology Conference (LTC): Human Language Technologies as a Challenge for Computer Science and Linguistics*, pages 227–231.

Yoav Seginer. 2007. Fast unsupervised incremental parsing. In *45th Annual Meeting of the Association of Computational Linguistics (ACL)*, pages 384–391.

Noah A. Smith and Jason Eisner. 2005. Guiding unsupervised grammar induction using contrastive estimation. In *IJCAI Workshop on Grammatical Inference Applications*, pages 73–82.

Valentin I. Spitkovsky, Hiyan Alshawi, and Daniel Jurafsky. 2009. Baby steps: How "Less is more" in unsupervised dependency parsing. In *NIPS 2009 Workshop on Grammar Induction, Representation of Language and Language Learning*.

Valentin I. Spitkovsky, Hiyan Alshawi, and Daniel Jurafsky. 2010a. From baby steps to leapfrog: How "Less is more" in unsupervised dependency parsing. In *Human Language Technologies: The 11th Annual Conference of the North American Chapter of the Association for Computational Linguistics (NAACL HLT 2010)*.

Valentin I. Spitkovsky, Daniel Jurafsky, and Hiyan Alshawi. 2010b. Profiting from Mark-Up: Hyper-Text annotations for guided parsing. In *48th Annual Meeting of the Association for Computational Linguistics (ACL 2010)*.

Valentin I. Spitkovsky, Hiyan Alshawi, Angel X Chang, and Daniel Jurafsky. 2011a. Unsupervised dependency parsing without gold Part-of-Speech tags. In *2011 Conference on Empirical Methods in Natural Language Processing (EMNLP 2011)*.

Valentin I. Spitkovsky, Hiyan Alshawi, and Daniel Jurafsky. 2011b. Lateen EM: unsupervised training with multiple objectives, applied to dependency grammar induction. In *2011 Conference on Empirical Methods in Natural Language Processing (EMNLP 2011)*.

Valentin I. Spitkovsky, Hiyan Alshawi, and Daniel Jurafsky. 2011c. Punctuation: Making a point in unsupervised dependency parsing. In *Fifteenth Conference on Computational Natural Language Learning (CoNLL-2011)*.

Kewei Tu and Vasant Honavar. 2011. On the utility of curricula in unsupervised learning of probabilistic grammars. In *22nd International Joint Conference on Artificial Intelligence (IJCAI 2011)*.

Dependency-Based Open Information Extraction

Pablo Gamallo and **Marcos Garcia**
Centro de Investigação sobre Tecnologias da Informação (CITIUS)
Universidade de Santiago de Compostela
pablo.gamallo@usc.es marcos.garcia.gonzalez@usc.es

Santiago Fernández-Lanza
Escola Superior de Enxeñería Informática
Universidade de Vigo
sflanzal@uvigo

Abstract

Building shallow semantic representations from text corpora is the first step to perform more complex tasks such as text entailment, enrichment of knowledge bases, or question answering. Open Information Extraction (OIE) is a recent unsupervised strategy to extract billions of basic assertions from massive corpora, which can be considered as being a shallow semantic representation of those corpora. In this paper, we propose a new multilingual OIE system based on robust and fast rule-based dependency parsing. It permits to extract more precise assertions (verb-based triples) from text than state of the art OIE systems, keeping a crucial property of those systems: scaling to Web-size document collections.

1 Introduction

There is an increasing interest in capturing shallow semantic representations from large amounts of text, with the aim of elaborating more complex semantic tasks involved in text understanding, such as textual entailment, filling knowledge gaps in text, or integration of text information into background knowledge bases. Two recent approaches to text understanding are interested in shallow semantics: Machine Reading (Etzioni et al., 2006) and Learning by Reading (Barker et al., 2007). Both approaches aim at understanding text by starting with a very basic representation of the facts conveyed by the input text. In addition, they rely on unsupervised strategies. There are, however, two significant differences between Machine Reading and Learning by Reading:

The first difference concerns the basic representation required at the beginning of the understanding process. While Machine Reading is focused on fixed structures (triples), constituted by a relation (a verb or verb phrase) and two arguments, in Learning by Reading the text is represented by means of more flexible predicate-argument structures (n-tuples) derived from syntactic dependency trees. In Learning by Reading, on the one hand, relations with more than two arguments are also extracted, and on the other, relations are not restricted to verb phrases but to whatever relation expressed by a dependency based triple, *(head, relation, modifier)*, also called Basic Element (Hovy et al., 2005). The second difference is related to the notion of text domain. Whereas Machine Reading works on open relations and unrestricted topics and domains, Learning by Reading prefers being focused on domain-specific texts in order to build a semantic model of a particular topic.

One of the major contributions of Machine Reading is the development of an extraction paradigm, called Open Information Extraction (OIE), which aims at extracting a large set of verb-based triples (or assertions) from unrestricted text. An OIE system reads in sentences and rapidly extracts one or more textual assertions, consisting in a verb relation and two arguments, which try to capture the main relationships in each sentence (Banko et al., 2007). Unlike most relation extraction methods which are focused on a predefined set of target relations, OIE is not limited to a small set of target relations known in advance, but extracts all types of (verbal) binary relations found in the text. The OIE system with best performance, called ReVerb (Etzioni et al., 2011), is a logistic regression classifier that takes as input PoS-tagged and NP-chunked sentences. So, it only requires shallow syntactic features to generate semantic relations, guaranteeing robustness and scalability with the size of the corpus. One of the main critics within the OIE paradigm against dependency based methods, such as Learning by Reading, concerns the computational cost associated with rich syntactic features. Dependency parsing could improve precision and recall over shallow syntactic features, but at the cost of extraction speed (Etzioni et al., 2011). In order to operate at the Web scale, OIE systems needs to be very fast and efficient.

In this paper, we describe an OIE method to generate verb-based triples by taking into account the positive properties of the two traditions: considering Machine Reading requirements, our system is efficient and fast guaranteeing scalability as the corpus grows. And considering ideas behind Learning by Reading, we use a dependency parser in order to obtain fine-grained information (e.g., internal heads and dependents) on the arguments and relations extracted from the text. In addition, we make extraction multilingual. More precisely, our system has the following properties:

- Unsupervised extraction of triples represented at different levels of granularity: surface forms and dependency level.
- Multilingual extraction (English, Spanish, Portuguese, and Galician) by making use of a multilingual rule-based parser, called DepPattern (Gamallo and González, 2011).

Our claim is that it is possible to perform Open Information Extraction by making use of very conventional tools, namely rule-based dependency analysis and simple post-processing extraction rules. In addition, we also show that we can deal with knowledge-rich syntactic information while remaining scalable.

This article is organized as follows. Section 2 introduces previous work on OIE: in particular it describes three of the best known OIE systems up to date. Next, in Section 3, the proposed method is described in detail. Then, some experiments are performed in Section 4, where our OIE system is compared against ReVerb. In 5, we sketch some applications that use the output of our OIE system, and finally, conclusions and current work are addressed in 6.

2 Open Information Extraction Systems

An OIE system extracts a large number of triples *(Arg1, Rel, Arg2)* for any binary relation found in the text. For instance, given the sentence "Vigo is the largest city in Galicia and is located in the northwest of Spain", an OIE system should extract two triples: *(Vigo, is the largest city in, Galicia)* and *(Vigo, is located in, northwest of Spain)*. Up to now, OIE is focused only on verb-based relations. Several OIE systems have been proposed, all of them are based on an extractor learned from labelled sentences. Some of these systems are:

- TextRunner (Banko et al., 2008): the extractor is a second order linear-chain CRF trained on samples of triples generated from the Penn Treebank. The input of TextRunner are PoS-tagged and NP-chunked sentences, both processes performed with OpenNLP tools.
- WOE (Wu and Weld, 2010): the extractor was learned by identifying the shortest dependency paths between two noun phrases, using training examples of Wikipedia. The main drawback is that extraction is 30 times slower than TextRunner.
- ReVerb (Etzioni et al., 2011; Fader et al., 2011): the extractor is a logistic regression classifier trained with shallow syntactic features, which also incorporates lexical constraints to filter out over-specified relation phrases. It takes as input the same features as TextRunner, i.e., PoS-tagged and NP-chunked sentences analyzed with OpenNLP tools. It is considered to be the best OIE system up to now. Its performance is 30% higher than WOE and more than twice that of TextRunner.

One of the most discussed problems of OIE systems is that about 90% of the extracted triples are not concrete facts (Banko et al., 2007) expressing valid information about one or two named entities, e.g. "Obama was born in Honolulu". However, the vast amount of high confident relational triples extracted by OIE systems are a very useful startpoint for further NLP tasks and applications, such as common sense knowledge acquisition (Lin et al., 2010), and extraction of domain-specific relations (Soderland et al.,

2010). The objective of OIE systems is not to extract concrete facts, but to transform unstructured texts into structured information, closer to ontology formats.

Nevertheless, some linguistics problems arise. OIE systems were trained to identify only verb clauses within the sentences and, therefore, to extract just binary verb-based relations from the clause structure. It follows that they cannot be easily adapted to learn other non-clausal relations also found in the text. Let us take the following sentence: "The soccer player of FC Barcelona, Lionel Messi, won the Fifa World Player of the Year award". In addition to the main verb-based relationship:

(Lionel Messi, won, the Fifa Worlds Player of the Year award)

which could be extracted by the OIE systems introduced above, it should also be important to extract other non-verbal relations found within the noun phrases:

(Messi, is, a soccer player of FC Barcelona)
(Fifa World Player of the Year, is, an award)

However, the cited systems were not trained to learn such a basic relations.

Besides, the OIE systems are not adapted to process clauses denoting events with many arguments. Take the sentence: "The first commercial airline flight was from St. Petersburg to Tampa in 1914". We should extract, at least, two or three different relational triples from the verb clause contained in this sentence, for instance:

(the first commercial airline flight, was from, St. Petersburg)
(the first commercial airline flight, was to, Tampa)
(the first commercial airline flight, was in, 1914)

Yet, current OIE systems are not able to perform this multiple extraction. Even if the cited OIE systems can identify several clauses per sentence, they were trained to only extract one triple per clause.

In the following, we will describe a dependency-based OIE system that overcomes these linguistic limitations.

3 A Dependency-Based Method for Open Information Extraction

The proposed extraction method consists of three steps organized as a chain of commands in a pipeline:

Dependency parsing Each sentence of the input text is analyzed using the dependency-based parser DepPattern, a multilingual tool available under GPL license[1].

Clause constituents For each parsed sentence, we discover the verb clauses it contains and, then, for each clause, we identify the verb participants, including their functions: subject, direct object, attribute, and prepositional complements.

Extraction rules A set of rules is applied on the clause constituents in order to extract the target triples.

These three steps are described in detail below.

3.1 Dependency Parsing

To parse text, we use an open-source suite of multilingual syntactic analysis, DepPattern (Gamallo and González, 2011). The suite includes basic grammars for five languages as well as a compiler to build parsers in Perl. A parser takes as input the output of a PoS-tagger, either, FreeLing (Carreras et al., 2004) or Tree-Tagger[2]. The whole process is robust and fast. It takes 2600 words per second on a Linux platform with 2.4GHz CPU and 2G memory. The basic grammars of DepPattern contain rules for many types of linguistic phenomena, from noun modification to more complex structures such as apposition or coordination. However their coverage is still not very high. We added several rules to the DepPattern grammars in English, Spanish, Portuguese, and Galician, in order to improve the coverage of our OIE system.

The output of a DepPattern parser consists of sentences represented as binary dependencies from the head lemma to the dependent lemma: *rel(head, dep)*. Consider the sentence "The coach of Benfica has held a press conference in Lisbon".

[1] `htpp://gramatica.usc.es/pln/tools/deppattern.htm`

[2] `http://www.ims.uni-stuttgart.de/projekte/corplex/TreeTagger/DecisionTreeTagger.html`

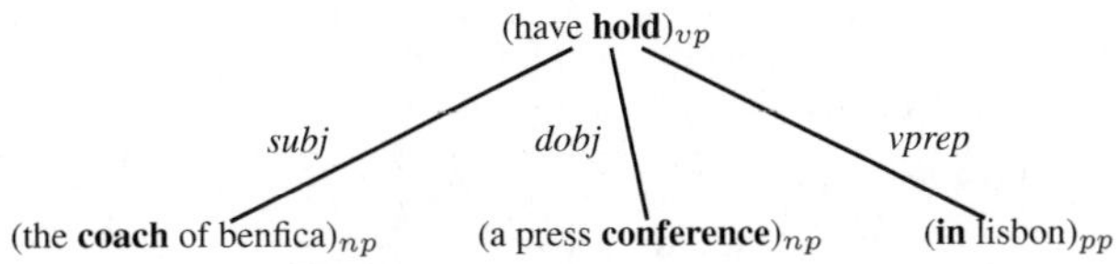

Figure 1: Constituency tree with function information

The DepPattern dependencies are the following:

spec(coach-2, the-1)
nprep(coach-2, of-3)
term(of-3, benfica-4)
aux(hold-6, have-5)
subj(hold-6, coach-2)
dobj(hold-6, conference-9)
spec(conference-9, a-7)
modif(conference-9, press-8)
vprep(hold-6, in-10)
term(in-10, lisbon-11)

The directed graph formed by these dependencies will be the input of the following step.

3.2 Clause Constituents

In the second step, we identify the clauses of each sentence, and, for each clause, we retain the participants and their functions with regard to the verb of the clause. A sentence can contain several clauses, in particular, we identify the main clause, relative clauses, and that-clauses.

In our example, there is just one clause constituted by a verb phrase (*"have hold"*) and three participants: the subject *"the coach of benfica"*, the direct object *"a press conference"*, and a prepositional phrase *"in lisbon"*. So, the objective here is to transform the dependency path built in the first step into a partial constituency tree, where only the constituents of the clause are selected. The process of constructing the clause constituents and the verb phrase is as follows.

Given a verb dependency (namely *subj*, *dobj*, *vprep*, or *attrib*), we select the dependent lemma of the clause verb and then we list all dependent lemmas linked to the target lemma (as a head) through the syntactic dependency path. It results in the construction of the main phrases of the clause, including information about the head of the phrase. We show below the three constituents identified from our example, where the directed arrows stand for the internal dependencies used for their identification (the head of each phrase is in bold):

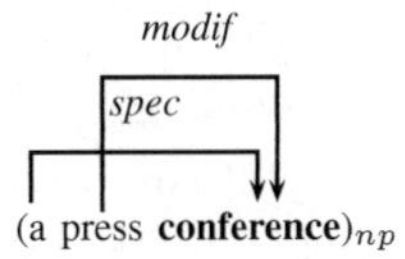

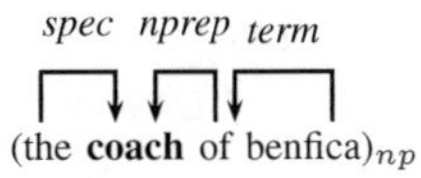

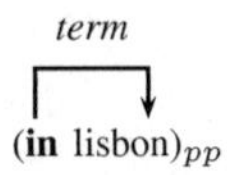

The verb phrase is also built in a similar way. It contains all dependent lemmas of the verb that are not part of the clause constituents identified before:

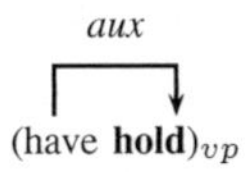

The three clause constituents are also provided with information about their function with regard to the clause verb, as Figure 1 shows. The function of a constituent inherits the name of the dependent relation linking the clause verb to the head of the constituent. For instance, the function of (the **coach** of benfica)$_{np}$ is the name of the dependent relation in *subj(hold-6, coach-2)*, that is *subj*. The clause constituents as well as the verb phrase of each clause are the input of the extraction rules.

3.3 Extraction Rules

The third and last process consists of a small set of simple extraction rules that are applied on the clauses identified in the previous step. The output of an extraction rule is a triple whose internal word tokens are provided with some linguistic information: lemma, PoS tag, head of the constituent, etc.

The simplest rule is applied on a clause just containing a subject and a direct object. In such a case, the two constituents are the arguments of the triple, while the verb phrase is the relation.

In our previous example, the clause contains three arguments: a subject (*"the coach of benfica"*), a direct object (*"a press conference"*), and a prepositional complement (*"in Lisbon"*). In this case, our strategy is similar to that of ReVerb system, namely to consider the relation as the verb phrase followed by a noun phrase and ending in a preposition. For this purpose, we have defined an extraction rule that builds the relation of the triple using the verb phrase, the direct object, and the head preposition of the prepositional phrase: *"have hold a press conference in"*. The two arguments are: *"the coach of benfica"* and *"Lisbon"*. The triple generated by our rule is represented as follows:

ARG1: *the_DT coach_N-H of_PRP benfica_N*
REL: *have_V hold_V-H a_DT press_N conference_N-H in_PRP*
ARG2: *Lisbon_N-H*

which contains lemmas, PoS tags (DT, N, PRP,...), as well as the heads (tag "H") of the main constituents. In addition to this syntax-based representation, the extraction rule also gives us a surface form of the triple with just tokens:

(the coach of Benfica, has hold a press conference in, Lisbon)

Table 1 shows the main rules we defined to extract triples from patterns of clause arguments. The order of arguments within a pattern is not relevant. The argument 'vprep' stands for a prepositional complement of the verb, which consists of a preposition and a nominal phrase (np). The third row represents the extraction rule used in our previous example. All rules in Table 1 are applied at different clause levels: main clauses, relative clauses and that-clauses.

As in the case of all current OIE systems, our small set of rules only considers verb-based clause triples and only extract one triple per clause. We took this decision in order to make a fair comparison when evaluating the performance of our system against ReVerb (in the next section). However, nothing prevents us from writing extraction rules to generate several triples from one clause with many arguments, or to extract triples from other patterns of constituents, for instance:

patterns	**triples**
subj-vp-dobj	Arg1 = subj Rel= vp Arg2 = dobj
subj-vp-vprep	Arg1 = subj Rel= vp+prep (prep from vprep) Arg2 = np (from vprep)
subj-vp-dobj-vprep	Arg1 = subj Rel= vp+dobj+prep Arg2 = np (from vprep)
subj-vp-attr	Arg1 = subj Rel= vp Arg2 = attr
subj-vp-attr-vprep	Arg1 = subj Rel= vp+attr+prep (from vprep) Arg2 = np (from vprep)

Table 1: Pattern based rules to generate final triples

vp-pp-pp, noun-prep-noun, noun-noun, adj-noun, or verb-adverb..

Finally, let us note that current OIE systems, such as ReVerb, produces triples only in textual, surface form. Substantial postprocessing is needed to derive relevant linguistic information from the tuples. By contrast, in addition to surface form triples, we also provide syntax-based information, PoS tags, lemmas, and heads. If more information is required, it can be easily obtained from the dependency analysis.

4 Experiments

4.1 Wikipedia Extraction

The system proposed in this paper, hereafter DepOE, was used to extract triples from the Wikipedia in four languages: Portuguese, Spanish, Galician, and English.[3] Before applying the extractor, the xml files containing the Wikipedia were properly converted into plaintext. The number of both sentences and extracted triples are shown in Table 2. We used PoS-tagged text with Tree-Tagger as input of DepPattern for the English extraction, and FreeLing for the other three languages. Note that, unlike OIE systems described in previous work, DepOE can be considered as being a multilingual OIE system.[4]

[3]Wikipedia dump files were downloaded at `http://download.wikipedia.org` on September 2010.

[4]DepOE is an open source system freely available, under GPL license, at `http://gramatica.usc.es/~gamallo/prototypes.htm`.

Wikipedia version	sentences	triples
English	78,826,696	47,284,799
Spanish	21,208,089	6,527,195
Portuguese	11,714,672	3,738,922
Galician	1,461,705	480,138

Table 2: Number of sentences and triples from four Wikipedias

It is worth mentioning that the number of extracted triples is lower than that obtained with ReVerb, which reaches 63,846,865 triples (without considering a threshold for confidence scores). This is due to the fact that the DepPattern grammars are not complete and, then, they do not perform deep analysis, just partial parsing. In particular, they do not consider all types of coordination and do not deal with significant linguistic clausal phenomena such as interrogative, conditional, causal, or adversative clauses. Preliminary evaluations of the four parsers showed that they behave in a similar way, yet Portuguese and Galician parsers achieve the best performance, about 70% f-score.

In this paper, we do not report experimental evaluation of the OIE system for languages other than English.

4.2 Evaluation

We compare Dep-OE to ReVerb[5], regarding the quantity and quality of extracted triples just in English, since ReVerb only can be applied on this language. Each system is given a set of sentences as input, and returns a set of triples as output. A test set of 200 sentences was created by randomly selecting sentences from the English Wikipedia. Each test sentence was independently examined by two judges in order to, on the one hand, identify the triples actually contained in the sentence, and on the other, evaluate each extraction as correct or incorrect. Incoherent and uninformative extractions were considered as incorrect. Given the sentence "The relationship between the Taliban and Bin Laden was close", an example of incoherent extraction is:

(Bin Laden, was, close)

Uninformative extractions occur when critical information is omitted, for instance, when one of the arguments is truncated. Given the sentence "FBI examined the relationship between Bin Laden and the Taliban", an OIE system could return a truncated triple:

(FBI, examined the relationship between, Bin Landen)

We follow similar criteria to those defined in previous OIE evaluations (Etzioni et al., 2011).

Concerning the decisions taken by the judges on the extractions made by the systems, the judges reached a very high agreement, 93%, with an agreement score of $\kappa = 0.83$. They also reached a high agreement, 86%, with regard to the number of triples (gold standard) found in the test sentences.

The precision of a system is the number of extractions returned as correct by the system divided by the number of returned extractions. Recall is the number of extractions returned as correct by the system divided by the number of triples identified by the judges (i.e., the size of the gold standard). Moreover, to compare our rule-based system DepOE to ReVerb, we had to select a particular threshold restricting the extractions made by ReVerb. Let us note that this extractor is a logistic regression classifier that assign confidence scores to its extractions. We computed precision and recall for many threshold and selected that giving rise to the best f-score. Such a threshold was 0.15. So, we compare DepOE to the results given by ReVerb for those extractions whose confidence score is higher than 0.15.

As it was done in previous OIE evaluations, the judges evaluated two different aspects of the extraction:

- how well the system identify correct relation phrases,
- the full extraction task, i.e., whether the system identifies correct triples (both the relation and its arguments).

Figures 2 and 3 represent the score average obtained by the two judges. They show that DepOE system is more precise than ReVerb. This is clear in the full extraction task, where DepOE achieves 68% precision while ReVerb reaches 52%. By contrast, as it was expected, DepOE has lower recall because of the low coverage of the grammars it depends on. Regarding f-score, DepOE

[5]`http://reverb.cs.washington.edu/`

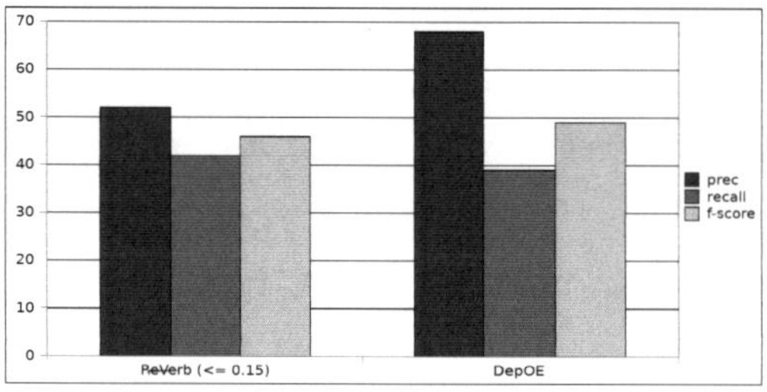

Figure 2: Evaluation of the extraction of triples (both relation and its arguments) performed by DepOE and ReVerb (with a confidence score $>= 0.15$).

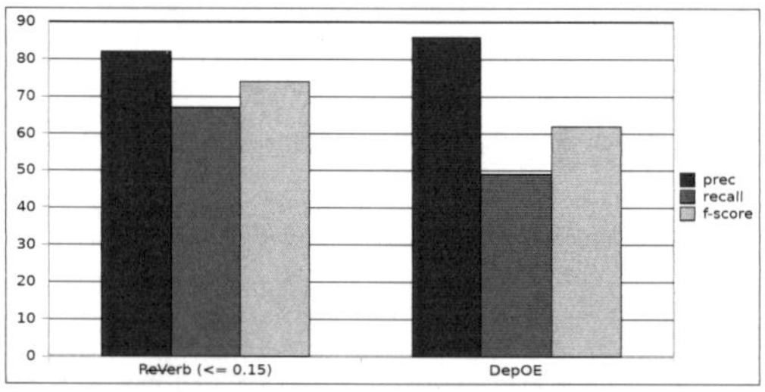

Figure 3: Evaluation of the relation extraction performed by DepOE and ReVerb (with a confidence score $>= 0.15$).

performs better than ReVerb in the full extraction task, but when only relations are considered, ReVerb achieves the highest score.

We found that most of the incorrect extractions returned by the two systems where cases where the relation phrase was correctly identified, but not one of the arguments. However, there are significant differences between the two systems concerning the type of problems arising in argument identification.

The most common errors of ReVerb are both: incorrect identification of the first argument (arg1) and extraction of only a truncated part of the second argument (arg2), as in the case of coordinating conjunctions. These two problems are crucial for ReVerb since more than 60% of incorrect extractions were cases with incorrect arguments and correct relations. DepOE has more precise extractions of the two arguments, in particular of arg1, since the parser is able to correctly identify the subject. Nevertheless, it also produces many truncated arg2. Let us see an example. Given the sentence "Cities and towns in Romania can have the status either of municipiu or oras", ReVerb was not able to identify the correct arg1 and returned a truncated arg2:

(Romania, can have, the status)

DepOE correctly identified the subject (arg1) but also failed to return the correct arg2:

(Cities and towns in Romania, can have, the status)

In general, when DepOE fails to correctly identify an argument, it is often trivial to find the reason of the problem. In the example above, arg2 was truncated because the English grammar has not any specific rule linking the particle "either" to a coordinate expression. So, the improvement of DepOE depends on improving the grammars it is based on. Besides the low coverage of the grammar, there are other sources of problems concerning the correct identification of arguments. In particular, it is worth mentioning that the English version of DepOE is not provided with an efficient Named Entity Recognition system. This makes it difficult to correctly identify multiword arguments with Named Entities, quantities, measures, and dates. Such a problem was partially solved by the use of FreeLing in the Portuguese, Spanish, and Galician DepOE versions.

4.3 Extraction Speed

To test the system's speed, we ran each extractor on the $100,000$ first lines of the English Wikipedia using a Linux platform with 2.4GHz CPU and 2GB memory. The processing time of ReVerb was 4 minutes while that of DepOE was 5 minutes and 19 seconds. In this platform, ReVerb is able to process $2,500$ words per second, and DepOE $1,650$. Concerning the use of RAM, ReVerb requires the 27% memory of the computer, while DepOE only needs 0.1%.

5 Applications

The extracted triples can be used for several NLP applications. The first application we are developing is a multilingual search engine over the triples extracted from the Wikipedia. All triples are indexed with Apache Solr[6], which enables it to rapidly answer queries regarding the extracted information, as in the query form of ReVerb[7].

Another application is to use the extracted triples to discover commonsense knowledge of

[6]http://lucene.apache.org/solr/

[7]http://textrunner.cs.washington.edu/reverb_demo.pl

team play game	
team win championship	
team win medal	
team win game	
team play match	
organism have DNA	
organism use energy	
organism recycle detritus	
organism respond to selection	
organism modify environment	

Table 3: Some of the most frequent basic propositions containing the words "team" and "organism", discovered by our system from Wikipedia.

specific domains. One of the goals of Learning by Reading is to enable a computer to acquire basic knowledge of different domains in order to improve question answering systems (Hovy et al., 2011). We assume that the head expressions of the most frequent triples extracted from a specific domain represent basic propositions (common knowledge) of that domain.

To check this assumption, we built two domain-specific corpora from Wikipedia: a corpus constituted by articles about sports, and another corpus with articles about Biology. Then, we extracted the triples from those corpora and, for each triple, we selected just the head words of its three elements: namely the main verb (and preposition if any) of the relation and the head nouns of the two arguments. It resulted in a list of basic propositions of a specific domain. Table 3 shows some of the propositions acquired following this method. They are some of the most frequent propositions containing two specific words, "team" and "organism", in the subject position (arg1) of the triples. The propositions with "team" were extracted from the corpus about sports, while those with "organism" were acquired from the corpus of Biology.

6 Conclusions and Current Work

We have described a multilingual Open Information Extraction method to extract verb-based triples from massive corpora. The method achieves better precision than state of the art systems, since it is based on deep syntactic information, namely dependency trees. In addition, given that dependency analysis is performed by fast, robust, and multilingual parsers, the method is scalable and applied to texts in several languages: we made experiments in English, Portuguese, Spanish, and Galician.

Our work shows that it is possible to perform Open Information Extraction by making use of knowledge-rich tools, namely rule-based dependency parsing and pattern-based extraction rules, while remaining scalable.

Even if in the experiments reported here we did not deal with relationships that are not binary, the use of deep syntactic information makes it easy to build n-ary relations from such cases, for instance complex events with internal (subject and object) and external (time and location) arguments: *"The treaty was signed by Portugal in 2003 in Lisbon"*. Furthermore, the use of deep syntactic information will also be useful to find important relationships that are not expressed by verbs. For instance, from the noun phrase *"Nobel Prize"*, we should extract the basic proposition: *(Nobel, is_a, prize)*.

In current work, we are working on synonymy resolution for two different cases found in the extracted triples: first, the case of multiple proper names for the same named entity and, second, the multiple ways a relationship can be expressed. Concerning the latter case, to solve relationship synonymy, we are making use of classic methods for relation extraction. Given a predefined set of target relations, a set of lexico-syntactic patterns is learned and used to identify those triples expressing the same relationship. This way, traditional closed information extraction could be perceived as a specific task aimed at normalizing and semantically organizing the results of open information extraction.

Acknowledgments

This work has been supported by the MICINN, within the projects with reference FFI2010-14986 and FFI2009-08828, as well as by *Diputación de Ourense* (INOU11A-04).

References

Michele Banko, Michael J Cafarella, Stephen Soderland, Matt Broadhead, and Oren Etzioni. 2007. Open information extraction from the web. In *International Joint Conference on Artificial Intelligence*.

Michele Banko, , and Oren Etzioni. 2008. The trade-offs between open and traditional relation extraction. In *Annual Meeting of the Association for Computational Linguistics*.

K. Barker, B. Agashe, S. Chaw, J. Fan, N. Friedland, M. Glass, J. Hobbs, E. Hovy, D. Israel, D.S. Kim, et al. 2007. Learning by reading: A prototype system, performance baseline and lessons learned. In *Proceeding of Twenty-Second National Conference of Artificial Intelligence (AAAI 2007)*.

X. Carreras, I. Chao, L. Padró, and M. Padró. 2004. An Open-Source Suite of Language Analyzers. In *4th International Conference on Language Resources and Evaluation (LREC'04)*, Lisbon, Portugal.

Oren Etzioni, Michele Banko, and Michael J. Cafarella. 2006. Machine reading. In *AAAI Conference on Artificial Intelligence*.

Oren Etzioni, Anthony Fader, Janara Christensen, Stephen Soderland, and Mausam. 2011. Open information extraction: the second generation. In *International Joint Conference on Artificial Intelligence*.

Anthony Fader, Stephen Soderland, and Oren Etzioni. 2011. Identifying relations for open information extraction. In *Conference on Empirical Methods in Natural Language Processing*.

Pablo Gamallo and Isaac González. 2011. A grammatical formalism based on patterns of part-of-speech tags. *International Journal of Corpus Linguistics*, 16(1):45–71.

Eduard Hovy, Chin yew Lin, and Liang Zhou. 2005. A BE-based Multi-document Summarizer with Sentence Compression. In *Proceedings of Multilingual Summarization Evaluation (ACL workshop). Ann Arbor, MI.*

Dirk Hovy, Chunliang Zhang, Eduard Hovy, and Anselmo Pe nas. 2011. Unsupervised discovery of domain-specific knowledge from text. In *Proceedings of 49th Annual Meeting of the Association for Computational Linguistics*, Portland, Oregon, USA.

Thomas Lin, Mausman, and Oren Etzioni. 2010. Identifying functional relations in web text. In *Conference on Empirical Methods in Natural Language Processing*.

Stephen Soderland, Brendan Roof, Bo Qin, Shi Xu, Mausam, and Oren Etzioni. 2010. Adapting open information extraction to domain-specific relations. *AI Magazine*, 31(3):93–102.

Fei Wu and Daniel S. Weld. 2010. Open information extraction using wikipedia. In *Annual Meeting of the Association for Computational Linguistics*.

Sweeping through the Topic Space: Bad luck? Roll again!

Martin Riedl and **Chris Biemann**
Ubiquitous Knowledge Processing Lab
Computer Science Department, Technische Universität Darmstadt
Hochschulstrasse 10, D-64289 Darmstadt, Germany
riedl@ukp.informatik.tu-darmstadt.de, biem@cs.tu-darmstadt.de

Abstract

Topic Models (TM) such as Latent Dirichlet Allocation (LDA) are increasingly used in Natural Language Processing applications. At this, the model parameters and the influence of randomized sampling and inference are rarely examined — usually, the recommendations from the original papers are adopted. In this paper, we examine the parameter space of LDA topic models with respect to the application of Text Segmentation (TS), specifically targeting error rates and their variance across different runs. We find that the recommended settings result in error rates far from optimal for our application. We show substantial variance in the results for different runs of model estimation and inference, and give recommendations for increasing the robustness and stability of topic models. Running the inference step several times and selecting the last topic ID assigned per token, shows considerable improvements. Similar improvements are achieved with the mode method: We store all assigned topic IDs during each inference iteration step and select the most frequent topic ID assigned to each word. These recommendations do not only apply to TS, but are generic enough to transfer to other applications.

1 Introduction

With the rise of topic models such as pLSI (Hofmann, 2001) or LDA (Blei et al., 2003) in Natural Language Processing (NLP), an increasing number of works in the field use topic models to map terms from a high-dimensional word space to a lower-dimensional semantic space. TMs are 'the new Latent Semantic Analysis' (LSA), (Deerwester et al., 1990), and it has been shown that generative models like pLSI and LDA not only have a better mathematical foundation rooted in probability theory, but also outperform LSA in document retrieval and classification, e.g. (Hofmann, 2001; Blei et al., 2003; Biro et al., 2008). To estimate the model parameters in LDA, the exact computation that was straightforward in LSA (matrix factorization) is replaced by a randomized Monte-Carlo sampling procedure (e.g. variational Bayes or Gibbs sampling).

Aside from the main parameter, the number of topics or dimensions, surprisingly little attention has been spent to understand the interactions of hyperparameters, the number of sampling iterations in model estimation and interference, and the stability of topic assignments across runs using different random seeds. While progress in the field of topic modeling is mainly made by adjusting prior distributions (e.g. (Sato and Nakagawa, 2010; Wallach et al., 2009)), or defining more complex model mixtures (Heinrich, 2011), it seems unclear whether improvements, reached on intrinsic measures like perplexity or on application-based evaluations, are due to an improved model structure or could originate from sub-optimal parameter settings or literally 'bad luck' due to the randomized nature of the sampling process.

In this paper, we address these issues by systematically sweeping the parameter space. For this, we pick LDA since it is the most commonly used TM in the field of NLP. To evaluate the contribution of the TM, we choose the task of TS: this task has received considerable interest from the NLP community, standard datasets and evaluation measures are available for testing, and it has been shown that this task considerably benefits from the use of TMs, see (Misra et al., 2009; Sun et al., 2008; Eisenstein, 2009).

This paper is organized as follows: In the next section, we present related work regarding text segmentation using topic models and topic model parameter evaluations. Section 3 defines the TopicTiling text segmentation algorithm, which is a simplified version of TextTiling (Hearst, 1994), and makes direct use of topic assignments. Its simplicity allows us to observe direct consequences of LDA parameter settings. Further, we describe the experimental setup, our application-based evaluation methodology including the data set and the LDA parameters we vary in Section 4.

Results of our experiments in Section 5 indicate that a) there is an optimal range for the number of topics, b) there is considerable variance in performance for different runs for both model estimation and inference, c) increasing the number of sampling iterations stabilizes average performance but does not make TMs more robust, but d) combining the output of several independent sampling runs does, and additionally leads to large error rate reductions. Similar results are obtained by e) the mode method with less computational costs using the most frequent topic ID that is assigned during different inference iteration steps. In the conclusion, we give recommendations to add stability and robustness for TMs: aside from optimization of the hyperparameters, we recommend combining the topic assignments of different inference iterations, and/or of different independent inference runs.

2 Related Work

2.1 Text Segmentation with Topic Models

Based on the observation of Halliday and Hasan (1976) that the density of coherence relations is higher within segments than between segments, most algorithms compute a coherence score to measure the difference of textual units for informing a segmentation decision. TextTiling (Hearst, 1994) relies on the simplest coherence relation – word repetition – and computes similarities between textual units based on the similarities of word space vectors. The task of text segmentation is to decide, for a given text, how to split this text into segments.

Related to our algorithm (see Section 3.1) are the approaches described in Misra et al. (2009) and Sun et al. (2008): topic modeling is used to alleviate the sparsity of word vectors by mapping words into a topic space. This is done by extending the dynamic programming algorithms from (Utiyama and Isahara, 2000; Fragkou et al., 2004) using topic models. At this, the topic assignments have to be inferred for each possible segment.

2.2 LDA and Topic Model Evaluation

For topic modeling, we use the widely applied LDA (Blei et al., 2003), This model uses a training corpus of documents to create document-topic and topic-word distributions and is parameterized by the number of topics T as well as by two hyperparameters. To generate a document, the topic proportions are drawn using a Dirichlet distribution with hyperparameter α. Adjacent for each word w a topic z_{d_w} is chosen according to a multinomial distribution using hyperparameter $\beta_{z_{d_w}}$. The model is estimated using m iterations of Gibbs sampling. Unseen documents can be annotated with an existing topic model using Bayesian inference methods. At this, Gibbs sampling with i iterations is used to estimate the topic ID for each word, given the topics of the other words in the same sentential unit. After inference, every word in every sentence receives a topic ID, which is the sole information that is used by the TopicTiling algorithm to determine the segmentation. We use the GibbsLDA implementation by Phan and Nguyen (2007) for all our experiments.

The article of Blei et al. (2003) compares LDA with pLSI and Mixture Unigram models using the perplexity of the model. In a collaborative filtering evaluation for different numbers of topics they observe that using too many topics leads to overfitting and to worse results.

In the field of topic model evaluations, Griffiths and Steyvers (2004) use a corpus of abstracts published between 1991 and 2001 and evaluate model perplexity. For this particular corpus, they achieve the lowest perplexity using 300 topics. Furthermore, they compare different sampling methods and show that the perplexity converges faster with Gibbs sampling than with expectation propagation and variational Bayes. On a small artificial testset, small variations in perplexity across different runs were observed in early sampling iterations, but all runs converged to the same limit.

In Wallach et al. (2009) topic models are evaluated with symmetric and asymmetric hyperparameters based on the perplexity. They observe a benefit using asymmetric parameters for α, but cannot show improvement with asymmetric priors for β.

3 Method

3.1 TopicTiling

For the evaluation of the topic models, a text segmentation algorithm called TopicTiling is used here. This algorithm is a newly developed algorithm based on TextTiling (Hearst, 1994) and achieves state of the art results using the Choi dataset, which is a standard dataset for TS evaluation. The algorithm uses sentences as minimal units. Instead of words, we use topic IDs that are assigned to each word using the LDA inference running on sentence units. The LDA model should be estimated on a corpus of documents that is similar to the to-be-segmented documents.

To measure the coherence c_p between two sentences around position p, the cosine similarity (vector dot product) between these two adjacent sentences is computed. Each sentence is represented as a T-dimensional vector, where T is the number of topic IDs defined in the topic model. The t-th element of the vector contains the number of times the t-th topic is observed in the sentence. Similar to the TextTiling algorithm, local minima calculated from these similarity scores are taken as segmentation candidates.

This is illustrated in Figure 1, where the similarity scores between adjacent sentences are plotted. The vertical lines in this plot indicate all local minima found.

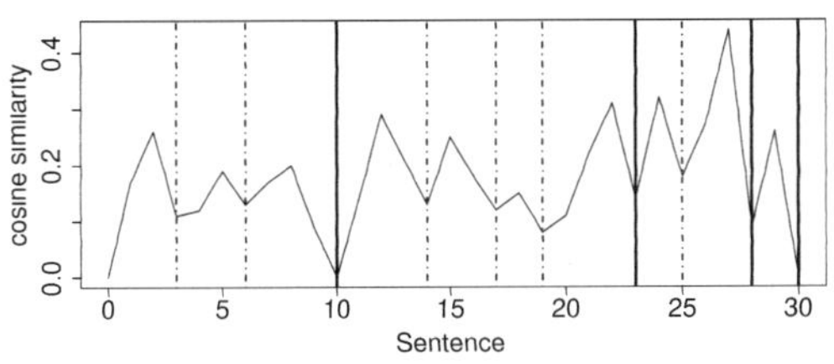

Figure 1: Cosine similarity scores of adjacent sentences based on topic distribution vectors. Vertical lines (solid and dashed) indicate local minima. Solid lines mark segments that have a depth score above a chosen threshold.

Following the TextTiling definition, not the minimum score c_p at position p itself is used, but a depth score d_p for position p computed by

$$d_i = 1/2 * (c_{p-1} - c_p + c_{p+1} - c_p). \quad (1)$$

In contrast to TextTiling, the directly neighboring similarity scores of the local minima are used, if they are higher than c_p. When using topics instead of words, it can be expected that sentences within one segment have many topics in common, which leads to cosine similarities close to 1. Further, using topic IDs instead of words greatly increases sparsity. A minimum in the curve indicates a change in topic distribution. Segment boundaries are set at the positions of the n highest depth-scores, which is common practice in text segmentation algorithms. An alternative to a given n would be the selection of segments according to a depth score threshold.

4 Experimental Setup

As dataset the Choi dataset (Choi, 2000) is used. This dataset is an artificially generated corpus that consists of 700 documents. Each document consists of 10 segments and each segment has 3–11 sentences extracted from a document of the Brown corpus. For the first setup, we perform a 10-fold Cross Validation (CV) for estimating the TM (estimating on 630 documents at a time), for the other setups we use 600 documents for TM estimation and the remaining 100 documents for testing. While we aim to neglect using the same documents for training and testing, it is not guaranteed that all testing data is unseen, since the same source sentences can find their way in several artificially crafted 'documents'. This problem, however, applies for all evaluations on this dataset that use any kind of training, be it LDA models in Misra et al. (2009) or TF-IDF values in Fragkou et al. (2004).

For the evaluation of the Topic Model in combination of Text Segmentation, we use the P_k measure (Beeferman et al., 1999), which is a standard measure for error rates in the field of TS. This measure compares the gold standard segmentation with the output of the algorithm. A P_k value of 0 indicates a perfect segmentation, the averaged state of the art on the Choi Dataset is $P_k = 0.0275$ (Misra et al., 2009). To assess the robustness of the TM, we sweep over varying configurations of the LDA model, and plot the results using Box-and-Whiskers plots: the box indicates the quartiles and the whiskers are maximal 1.5 times of the Interquartile Range (IQR) or equal to the data point that is no greater to the 1.5 IQR. The following parameters are subject to our exploration:

- T: Number of topics used in the LDA model. Common values vary between 50 and 500.
- α : Hyperparameter that regulates the sparseness topic-per-document distribution. Lower values result in documents being represented by fewer topics (Heinrich, 2004). Recommended: $\alpha = 50/T$ (Griffiths and Steyvers, 2004)
- β : Reducing β increases the sparsity of topics, by assigning fewer terms to each topic, which is correlated to how related words need to be, to be assigned to a topic (Heinrich, 2004). Recommended: $\beta = \{0.1, 0.01\}$ (Griffiths and Steyvers, 2004; Misra et al., 2009)
- m Model estimation iterations. Recommended / common settings: $m = 500-5000$ (Griffiths and Steyvers, 2004; Wallach et al., 2009; Phan and Nguyen, 2007)
- i Inference iterations. Recommended / common settings: 100 (Phan and Nguyen, 2007)
- d Mode of topic assignments. At each inference iteration step, a topic ID is assigned to each word within a document (represented as a sentence in our application). With this option, we count these topic assignments for each single word in each iteration. After all i inference iterations, the most frequent topic ID is chosen for each word in a document.
- r Number of inference runs: We repeat the inference r times and assign the most frequently assigned topic per word at the final inference run for the segmentation algorithm. High r values might reduce fluctuations due to the randomized process and lead to a more stable word-to-topic assignment.

All introduced parameters parameterize the TM. We are not aware of any research that has used several inference runs r and the mode of topic assignments d to increase stability and varying TM parameters in combinations with measures other then perplexity.

5 Results

In this section, we present the results we obtained from varying the parameters under examination.

5.1 Number of Topics T

To provide a first impression of the data, a 10-fold CV is calculated and the segmentation results are visualized in Figure 2.

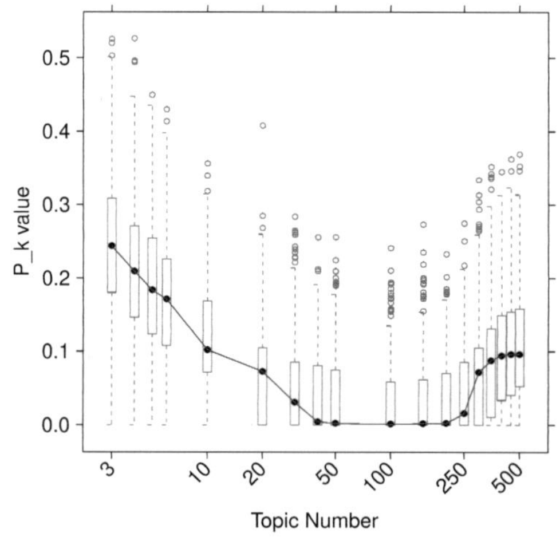

Figure 2: Box plots for different number of topics T. Each box plot is generated from the average P_k value of 700 documents, $\alpha = 50/T$, $\beta = 0.1$, $m = 1000$, $i = 100, r = 1$. These documents are segmented with TopicTiling using a 10-folded CV.

Each box plot is generated from the P_k values of 700 documents. As expected, there is a continuous range of topic numbers, namely between 50 and 150 topics, where we observe the lowest P_k values. Using too many topics leads to overfitting of the data and too few topics result in too general distinctions to grasp text segments. This is in line with other studies, that determine an optimum for T, cf. (Griffiths and Steyvers, 2004), which is specific to the application and the data set.

5.2 Estimation and Inference iterations

The next step examines the robustness of the topic model according to the number of model estimation iterations m needed to achieve stable results. 600 documents are used to train the LDA model that is applied by TopicTiling to segment the remaining 100 documents. From Figure 2 we know that sampling 100 topics leads to good results. To have an insight into unstable topic regions we also inspect performance at different sampling iterations using 20 and 250 topics. To assess stability across different model estimation runs, we trained 30 LDA models using different random seeds. Each box plot in Figures 3 and 4 is generated from 30 mean values, calculated from the P_k values of the 100 documents. The variation indicates the score variance for the 30 different models.

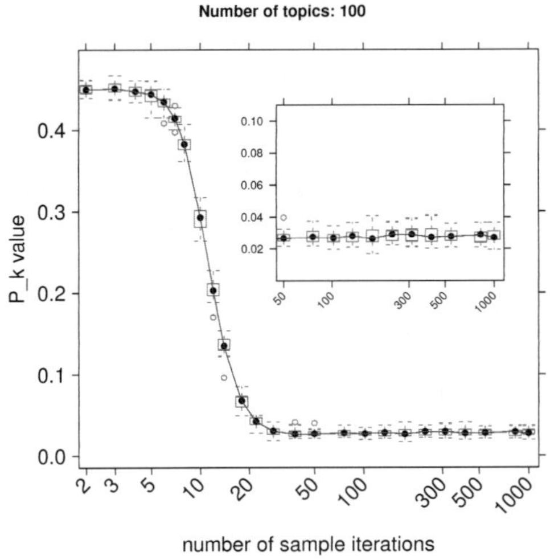

Figure 3: Box plots with different model estimation iterations m, with T=100, $\alpha = 50/T$, $\beta = 0.1$, $i = 100$, $r = 1$. Each box plot is generated from 30 mean values calculated from 100 documents.

Using 100 topics (see Figure 3), the burn-in phase starts with 8–10 iterations and the mean P_k values stabilize after 40 iterations. But looking at the inset for large m values, significant variations between the different models can be observed: note that the P_k error rates are almost double between the lower and the upper whisker. These remain constant and do not disappear for larger m values: The whiskers span error rates between 0.021 - 0.037 for model estimation on document units

With 20 topics, the P_k values are worse as with 100 topics, as expected from Figure 2. Here the convergence starts at 100 sample iterations. More interesting results are achieved with 250 topics. A robust range for the error rates can be found between 20 and 100 sample iterations. With more iterations m, the results get both worse and unstable: as the 'natural' topics of the collection have to be split in too many topics in the model, perplexity optimizations that drive the estimation process lead to random fluctuations, which the TopicTiling algorithm is sensitive to. Manual inspection of models for $T = 250$ revealed that in fact many topics do not stay stable across estimation iterations.

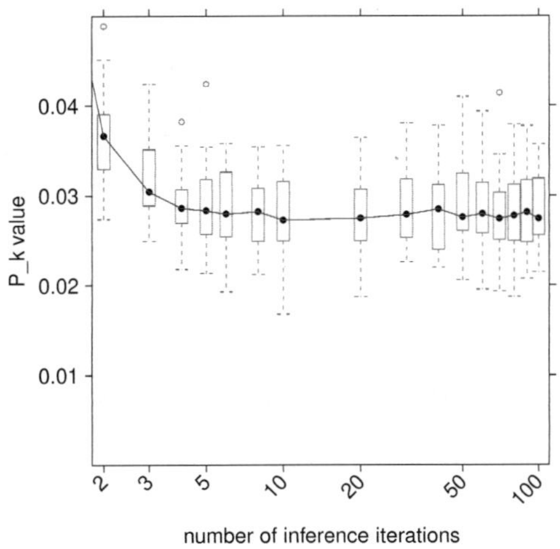

Figure 5: Figure of box plots for different inference iterations i and $m = 1000$, $T = 100$, $\alpha = 50/T$, $\beta = 0.1$, $r = 1$.

In the next step we sweep over several inference iterations i. Starting from 5 iterations, error rates do not change much, see Figure 5. But there is still substantial variance, between about 0.019 - 0.038 for inference on sentence units.

5.3 Number of inference runs r

To decrease this variance, we assign the topic not only from a singe inference run, but repeat the inference calculations several times, denoted by the parameter r. Then the frequency of assigned topic IDs per token is counted across the r runs, and we assign the most frequent topic ID (frequency ties are broken randomly). The box plot for several evaluated values of r is shown in Figure 6.

This log-scaled plot shows that both variance and P_k error rate can be substantially decreased. Already for $r = 3$, we observe a significant improvement in comparison to the default setting of $r = 1$ and with increasing r values, the error rates are reduced even more: for $r = 20$, variance and error rates are is cut in less than half of their original values using this simple operation.

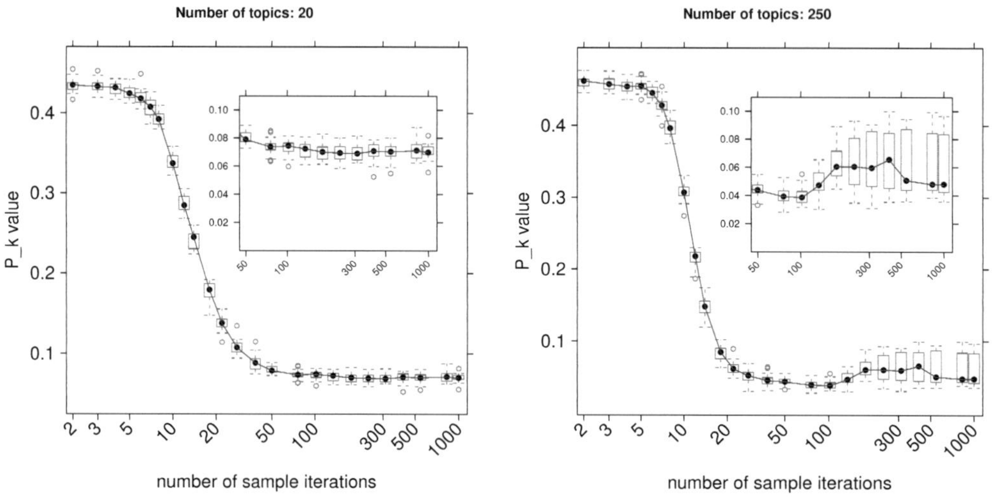

Figure 4: Box plots with varying model estimation iterations m applied with $T = 20$ (left) and $T = 250$ (right) topics, $\alpha = 50/T$, $\beta = 0.1$, $i = 100$, $r = 1$

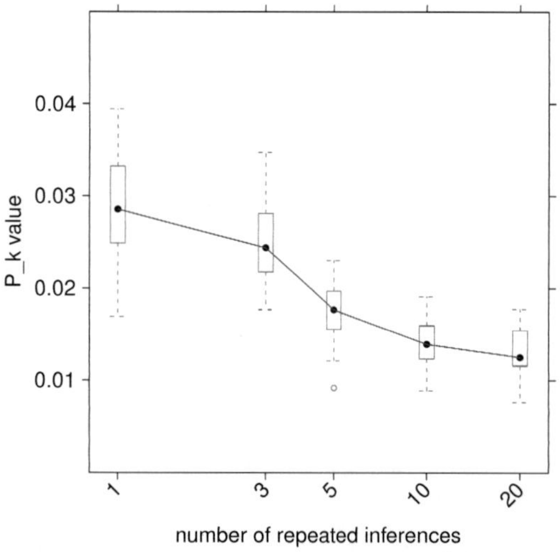

Figure 6: Box plot for several inference runs r, to assign the topics to a word with $m = 1000$, $i = 100$, $T = 100$, $\alpha = 50/T$, $\beta = 0.1$.

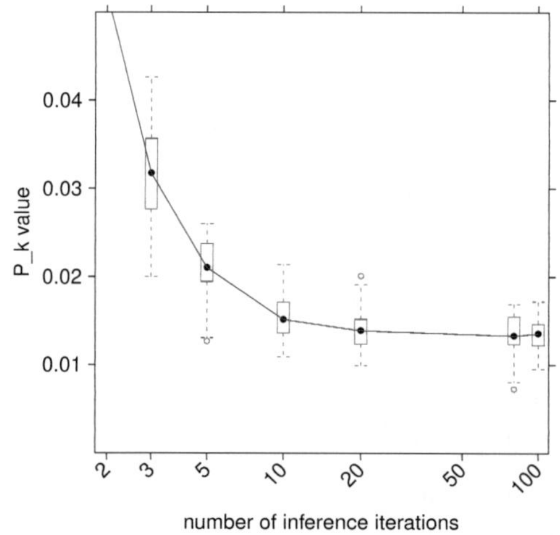

Figure 7: Box plot using the mode method $d = true$ with several inference iterations i with $m = 500$, $T = 100$, $\alpha = 50/T$, $\beta = 0.1$.

5.4 Mode of topic assignment d

In the previous experiment, we use the topic IDs that have been assigned most frequently at the last inference iteration step. Now, we examine something similar, but for all i inference steps of a single inference run: we select the mode of topic ID assignments for each word across all inference steps. The impact of this method on error and variance is illustrated in Figure 7. Using a single inference iteration, the topic IDs are almost assigned randomly. After 20 inference iterations P_k values below 0.02 are achieved. Using further iterations, the decrease of the error rate is only marginal. In comparison to the repeated inference method, the additional computational costs of this method are much lower as the inference iterations have to be carried out anyway in the default application setting.

5.5 Hyperparameters α and β

In many previous works, hyperparameter settings $\alpha = 50/T$ and $\beta = \{0.1, 0.01\}$ are commonly used. In the next series of experiments we investigate how different parameters of these both parameters can change the TS task.

For α values, shown in Figure 8, we can see that the recommended value for $T = 100$, $\alpha =$

0.5 leads to sub-optimal results, and an error rate reduction of about 40% can be realized by setting $\alpha = 0.1$.

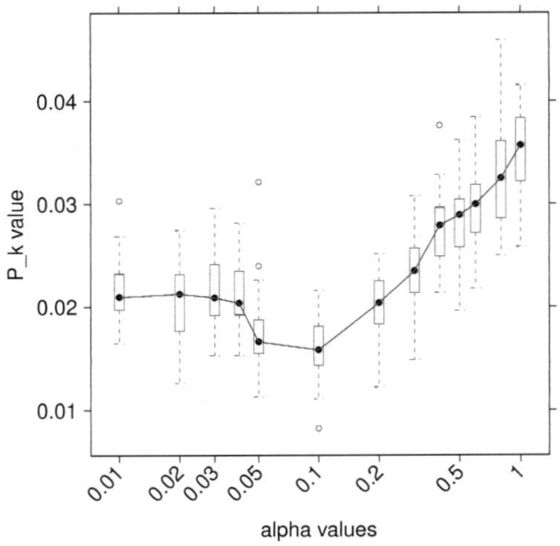

Figure 8: Box plot for several alpha values α with $m = 500$, $i = 100$, $T = 100$, $\beta = 0.1$, $r = 1$.

Regarding values of β, we find that P_k rates and their variance are relatively stable between the recommended settings of 0.1 and 0.01. Values larger than 0.1 lead to much worse performance. Regarding variance, no patterns within the stable range emerge, see Figure 9.

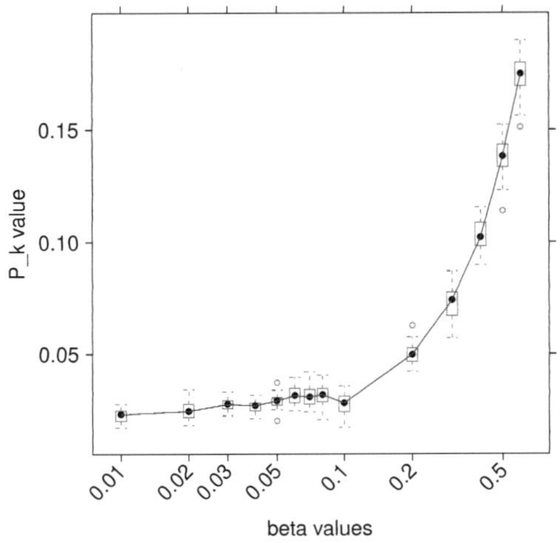

Figure 9: Box plot for several beta values β with $m = 500$, $i = 100$, $T = 100$, $\alpha = 50/T$, $r = 1$.

5.6 Putting it all together

Until this point, we have examined different parameters with respect to stability and error rates one at the time. Now, we combine what we have learned from this and strive at optimal system performance. For this, we contrast TS results obtained with the default LDA configuration with the best systems obtained by optimization of single parameters, as well as to a system that uses these optimal settings for all parameters. Table 1 shows P_k error rates for the different systems. At this, we fixed the following parameters: $T = 100$, $m = 500$, $i = 100$, $\beta = 0.1$. For the computations we use 600 documents for the LDA model estimation, apply TopicTiling and compute the error rate for the 100 remaining documents and repeat this 30 times with different random seeds.

System	P_k	error red.	σ^2	var. red.
default	0.0302	0.00%	2.02e-5	0.00%
$\alpha = 0.1$	0.0183	39.53%	1.22e-5	39.77%
$r = 20$	0.0127	57.86%	4.65e-6	76.97%
$d = true$	0.0137	54.62%	3.99e-6	80.21%
combined	0.0141	53.45%	9.17e-6	54.55%

Table 1: Comparison of single parameter optimizations, and combined system. P_k averages and variance are computed over 30 runs, together with reductions relative to the default setting. Default: $\alpha = 0.5$, $r = 1$. combined: $\alpha = 0.1$, $r = 20$, $d = true$

We can observe a massive improvement for optimized single parameters. The α-tuning tuning results in an error rate reduction of 39.77% in comparison to the default configurations. Using $r = 20$, the error rate is cut in less than half its original value. Also for the mode mechanism ($d = true$) the error rate is halved but slightly worse than than when using the repeated inference. Using combined optimized parameters does not result to additional error decreases. We attribute the slight decline of the combined method in both in the error rate P_k and in the variance to complex parameter interactions that shall be examined in further work. In Figure 10, we visualize these results in a density plot. It becomes clear that repeated inference leads to slightly better and more robust performance (higher peak) than the mode method. We attribute the difference to situations, where there are several highly probable topics in our sampling units, and by chance the same one is picked for adjacent sentences that belong to different segments, resulting in failure to recognize the segmentation point. However, since the differences are miniscule, only using the mode method might be more suitable for practical purposes since its computational cost is lower.

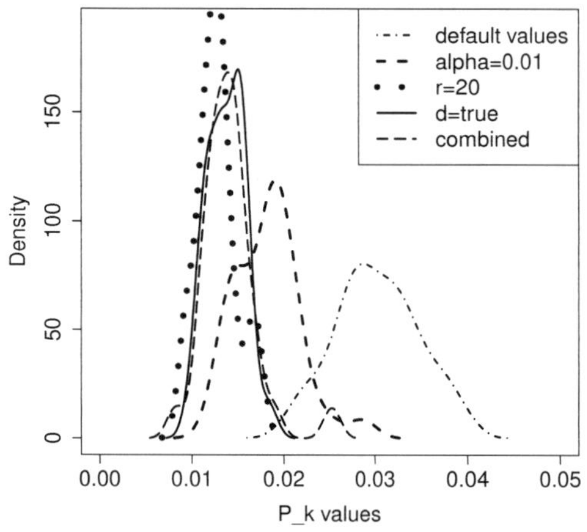

Figure 10: Density plot of the error distributions for the systems listed in Table 1

6 Conclusion

In this paper, we examined the robustness of LDA topic models with respect to the application of Text Segmentation by sweeping through the topic model parameter space. To our knowledge, this is the first attempt to systematically assess the stability of topic models in a NLP task.

The results of our experiments are summarized as follows:

- Perform the inference r times using the same model and choosing the assigned topic ID per word token taken from the last inference iteration, improves both error rates and stability across runs with different random seeds.

- Almost equal performance in terms of error and stability is achieved with the mode mechanism: choose the most frequent topic ID assignment per word across inference steps. While error rates were slightly higher for our data set, this method is probably preferable in practice because of its lower computation costs.

- As found in other studies, there is a range for the number of topics T, where optimal results are obtained. In our task, performance showed to be robust in the range of 50 - 150 topics.

- The default setting for LDA hyperparameters α and β can lead to sub-optimal results. Especially α should be optimized for the task at hand, as the utility of the topic model is very sensitive to this parameter.

- While the number of iterations for model estimation and inference needed for convergence is depending on the number of topics, the size of the sampling unit (document) and the collection, it should be noted that after convergence the variance between different sampling runs does not decrease for a larger number of iterations.

Equipped with the insights gained from experiments on single parameter variation, we were able to implement a very simple algorithm for text segmentation that improves over the state of the art on a standard dataset by a large margin. At this, the combination of the optimal α, and a high number of inference repetitions r and the mode method ($d = true$) produced slightly more errors than a high r alone. While the purpose of this paper was mainly to address robustness and stability issues of topic models, we are planning to apply the segmentation algorithm to further datasets.

The most important takeaway, however, is that especially for small sampling units like sentences, tremendous improvements in applications can be obtained when looking at multiple inference assignments and using the most frequently assigned topic ID in subsequent processing – either across diffeent inference steps or across diffeent inference runs. These two new strategies seem to be able to offset sub-optimal hyperparameters to a certain extent. This scheme is not only applicable to Text Segmentation, but in all applications where performance crucially depends on stable topic ID assignments per token. Extensions to this scheme, like ignoring tokens with a high topic variability (stop words or general terms) or dynamically deciding to conflate several topics because of their per-token co-occurrence, are left for future work.

7 Acknowledgments

This work has been supported by the Hessian research excellence program "Landes-Offensive zur Entwicklung Wissenschaftlich-konomischer Exzellenz" (LOEWE) as part of the research center "Digital Humanities". We would also thank the anonymous reviewers for their comments, which greatly helped to improve the paper.

References

D. Beeferman, A. Berger, and J. Lafferty. 1999. Statistical models for text segmentation. *Machine learning*, 34(1):177–210.

Istvan Biro, Andras Benczur, Jacint Szabo, and Ana Maguitman. 2008. A comparative analysis of latent variable models for web page classification. In *Proceedings of the 2008 Latin American Web Conference*, pages 23–28, Washington, DC, USA. IEEE Computer Society.

David M. Blei, Andrew Y. Ng, and Michael I. Jordan. 2003. Latent dirichlet allocation. *J. Mach. Learn. Res.*, 3:993–1022, March.

Freddy Y. Y. Choi. 2000. Advances in domain independent linear text segmentation. In *Proceedings of the 1st North American chapter of the Association for Computational Linguistics conference*, NAACL 2000, pages 26–33, Stroudsburg, PA, USA. Association for Computational Linguistics.

Scott Deerwester, Susan T. Dumais, George W. Furnas, Thomas K. Landauer, and Richard Harshman. 1990. Indexing by latent semantic analysis. *Journal of the American Society for Information Science*, 41(6):391–407.

Jacob Eisenstein. 2009. Hierarchical text segmentation from multi-scale lexical cohesion. *Proceedings of Human Language Technologies: The 2009 Annual Conference of the North American Chapter of the Association for Computational Linguistics on - NAACL '09*, page 353.

P. Fragkou, V. Petridis, and Ath. Kehagias. 2004. A Dynamic Programming Algorithm for Linear Text Segmentation. *Journal of Intelligent Information Systems*, 23(2):179–197, September.

Thomas L. Griffiths and Mark Steyvers. 2004. Finding scientific topics. *PNAS*, 101(suppl. 1):5228–5235.

M A K Halliday and Ruqaiya Hasan. 1976. *Cohesion in English*, volume 1 of *English Language Series*. Longman.

Marti a. Hearst. 1994. Multi-paragraph segmentation of expository text. *Proceedings of the 32nd annual meeting on Association for Computational Linguistics*, (Hearst):9–16.

Gregor Heinrich. 2004. Parameter estimation for text analysis. Technical report.

Gregor Heinrich. 2011. Typology of mixed-membership models: Towards a design method. In *Machine Learning and Knowledge Discovery in Databases*, volume 6912 of *Lecture Notes in Computer Science*, pages 32–47. Springer Berlin / Heidelberg. 10.1007/978-3-642-23783-6 3.

Thomas Hofmann. 2001. Unsupervised Learning by Probabilistic Latent Semantic Analysis. *Computer*, pages 177–196.

Hemant Misra, Joemon M Jose, and Olivier Cappé. 2009. Text Segmentation via Topic Modeling : An Analytical Study. In *Proceeding of the 18th ACM Conference on Information and Knowledge Management - CIKM '09*, pages 1553—-1556.

Xuan-Hieu Phan and Cam-Tu Nguyen. 2007. GibbsLDA++: A C/C++ implementation of latent Dirichlet allocation (LDA). http://jgibblda.sourceforge.net/.

Issei Sato and Hiroshi Nakagawa. 2010. Topic models with power-law using pitman-yor process categories and subject descriptors. *Science And Technology*, (1):673–681.

Qi Sun, Runxin Li, Dingsheng Luo, and Xihong Wu. 2008. Text segmentation with LDA-based Fisher kernel. *Proceedings of the 46th Annual Meeting of the Association for Computational Linguistics on Human Language Technologies Short Papers - HLT '08*, (June):269.

Masao Utiyama and Hitoshi Isahara. 2000. A Statistical Model for Domain-Independent Text Segmentation. *Communications*.

Hanna Wallach, David Mimno, and Andrew McCallum. 2009. Rethinking lda: Why priors matter. In *NIPS*.

Clustered Word Classes for Preordering in Statistical Machine Translation

Sara Stymne
Linköping University, Sweden
sara.stymne@liu.se

Abstract

Clustered word classes have been used in connection with statistical machine translation, for instance for improving word alignments. In this work we investigate if clustered word classes can be used in a preordering strategy, where the source language is reordered prior to training and translation. Part-of-speech tagging has previously been successfully used for learning reordering rules that can be applied before training and translation. We show that we can use word clusters for learning rules, and significantly improve on a baseline with only slightly worse performance than for standard POS-tags on an English–German translation task. We also show the usefulness of the approach for the less-resourced language Haitian Creole, for translation into English, where the suggested approach is significantly better than the baseline.

1 Introduction

Word order differences between languages are problematic for statistical machine translation (SMT). If the word orders of two languages have large differences, the standard methods do not tend to work well, with difficulties in many steps such as word alignment and modelling of reordering in the decoder. This can be addressed by applying a preordering method, that is, to reorder the source side of the corpus to become similar to the target side, prior to training and translation. The rules used for reordering are generally based on some kind of linguistic annotation, such as part-of-speech tags (POS-tags).

For many languages in the world, so called less-resourced languages, however, part-of-speech taggers, or part-of-speech tagged corpora that can be used for training a tagger, are not available. In this study we investigate if it is possible to use unsupervised POS-tags, in the form of clustered word classes, as a basis for learning reordering rules for SMT. Unsupervised tagging methods can be used for any language where a corpus is available. This means that we can potentially benefit from preordering even for languages where taggers are available.

We present experiments on two data sets. First an English–German test set, where we can compare the results of clustered word classes with standard tags. We show that both types of tags beat a baseline without preordering, and that clustered tags perform nearly as well as standard tags. English and German is an interesting case for reordering experiments, since there are both long distance movement of verbs and local word order differences, for instance due to differences in adverb placements. We also apply the method to translation from the less-resourced language Haitian Creole into English, and show that it leads to an improvement over a baseline. The differences in word order between these two languages are smaller than for English–German.

Besides potentially improving SMT for less-resourced languages, the presented approach can also be used as an extrinsic evaluation method for unsupervised POS-tagging methods. This is especially useful for the task of word class clustering which is hard to evaluate.

2 Unsupervised POS-tagging

There have been several suggestions of clustering methods for obtaining word classes that are completely unsupervised, and induce classes from raw text. Brown et al. (1992) described a hierarchical word clustering method which maximizes the mutual information of bigrams. Schütze (1995) described a distributional clustering algorithm that uses global context vectors as a basis for clustering. Biemann (2006) described a graph-based clustering methods for word classes. Goldwater and Griffiths (2007) used Bayesian reasoning for word class induction. Och (1999) described a method for determining bilingual word classes, used to improve the extraction of alignment templates through alignments between classes, not only between words. He also described a monolingual word clustering method, which is based on a maximum likelihood approach, using the frequencies of unigrams and bigrams in the training corpus.

The above methods are fully unsupervised, and produce unlabelled classes. There has also been work on what Goldwater and Griffiths (2007) call POS disambiguation, where the learning of classes is constrained by a dictionary of the allowable tags for each word. Such work has for instance been based on hidden Markov models (Merialdo, 1994), log-linear models (Smith and Eisner, 2005), and Bayesian reasoning (Goldwater and Griffiths, 2007).

Word clusters have previously been used for SMT for improving word alignment (Och, 1999), in a class-based language model (Costa-jussà et al., 2007) or for extracting gappy patterns (Gimpel and Smith, 2011). To the best of our knowledge this is the first study of applying clustered word classes for creating pre-translation reordering rules. The most similar work we are aware of is Costa-jussà and Fonollosa (2006) who used clustered word classes in a strategy they call statistical machine reordering, where the corpus is translated into a reordered language using standard SMT techniques in a pre-processing step. The addition of word classes led to improvements over just using surface form, but no comparison to using POS-tags were shown. Clustered word classes have also been used in a discriminate reordering model (Zens and Ney, 2006), and were shown to reduce the classification error rate.

Word clusters have also been used for unsupervised and semi-supervised parsing. Klein and Manning (2004) used POS-tags as the basis of a fully unsupervised parsing method, both for dependency and constituency parsing. They showed that clustered word classes can be used instead of conventional POS-tags, with some result degradation, but that it is better than several baseline systems. Koo et al. (2008) used features based on clustered word classes for semi-supervised dependency parsing and showed that using word class features together with POS-based features led to improvements, but using word class features instead of POS-based features only degraded results somewhat.

3 Reordering for SMT

There is a large amount of work on reordering for statistical machine translation. One way to approach reordering is by extending the translation model, either by adding extra models, such as lexicalized (Koehn et al., 2005) or discriminative (Zens and Ney, 2006) reordering models or by directly modelling reordering in hierarchical (Chiang, 2007) or syntactical translation models (Yamada and Knight, 2002).

Preordering is another common strategy for handling reordering. Here the source side of the corpus is transformed in a preprocessing step to become more similar to the target side. There have been many suggestions of preordering strategies. Transformation rules can be handwritten rules targeting known syntactic differences (Collins et al., 2005; Popović and Ney, 2006), or they can be learnt automatically (Xia and McCord, 2004; Habash, 2007). In these studies the reordering decision was taken deterministically on the source side. This decision can be delayed to decoding time by presenting several reordering options to the decoder as a lattice (Zhang et al., 2007; Niehues and Kolss, 2009) or as an n-best list (Li et al., 2007).

Generally reordering rules are applied to the source language, but there have been attempts at target side reordering as well (Na et al., 2009). Reordering rules can be based on different levels of linguistic annotation, such as POS-tags (Niehues and Kolss, 2009), chunks (Zhang et al., 2007) or parse trees (Xia and McCord, 2004). Common for all these levels is that a tool like a tagger or parser is needed for them to work.

In all the above studies, the reordering rules are applied to the translation input, but they are only applied to the training data in a few cases, for instance in Popović and Ney (2006). Rottmann and Vogel (2007) compared two strategies for reordering the training corpus, by using alignments, and by applying the reordering rules to create a lattice from which they extracted the 1-best reordering. They found that it was better to use the latter option, to reorder the training data based on the rules, than to use the original order in the training data. Using alignment-based reordering was not successful, however. Another option for using reorderings in the training data was presented by Niehues et al. (2009), who directly extracted phrase pairs from reordering lattices, and showed a small gain over non-reordered training data.

3.1 POS-based Preordering

Our work is based on the POS-based reordering model described by Niehues and Kolss (2009), in which POS-based rules are extracted from a word aligned corpus, where the source side is part-of-speech tagged. There are two types of rules. Short-range rules (Rottmann and Vogel, 2007) contain a pattern of POS-tags, and a possible reordering to resemble the target language, such as `VVIMP VMFIN PPER` → `PPER VMFIN VVIMP`, which moves a personal pronoun to a position in front of a verb group. Long-range rules were designed to cover movements over large spans, and also contain gaps that can match one or several words, such as `VAFIN * VVPP` → `VAFIN VVPP *`, which moves the two parts of a German verbs together past an object of any size, so as to resemble English.

Short-range rules are extracted by identifying POS-sequences in the training corpus where there are crossing alignments. The rules are stored as the part-of-speech pattern of the source on the left hand side of the rule, and the pattern corresponding to the target side word order on the right hand side.

Long-range rules are extracted in a similar way, by identifying two neighboring POS-sequences on the source side that have crossed alignments. Gaps are introduced into the rules by replacing either the right hand side or the left hand side by a wild card. In order to constrain the application of these rules, the POS-tag to the left of the rule is included in the rule. Depending on the language pair it might be advantageous to use rules that have wildcards either on the left or right hand side. For German-to-English translation, the main long distance movement is that verbs move to the left, and, as shown by Niehues and Kolss (2009), it is advantageous to use only long-range rules with left-wildcards, as in the example rule above. For the other translation direction, it is important to move verbs to the right, and thus right-wildcard rules were better.

The probability of both short and long range rules is calculated by relative frequencies as the number of times a rule occurs divided by the number of times the source side occurs in the training data.

In a preprocessing step to decoding, all rules are applied to each input sentence, and when a rule applies, the alternative word order is added to a word lattice. To keep lattices of a reasonable size, Niehues and Kolss (2009) suggested using a threshold of 0.2 for the probability of short-range rules, of 0.05 for the probability of long range rules, and blocked rules that could be applied more than 5 times to the same sentence. We adopt these threshold values.

In this work we use the short-range reordering rules of Rottmann and Vogel (2007) and the long-range rules of Niehues and Kolss (2009). As suggested we use only right-wildcard rules for English–German translation. For Haitian Creole, we have no prior knowledge of the reordering direction, and thus choose to use both left and right long-range rules. In previous work only one standard POS-tagset was explored. In this work we investigate the effect of different type of annotation schemes, besides only POS-tags. We use several types of tags from a parser, and compare them to using unsupervised tags in the form of clustered word classes. We also apply the reordering techniques to translation from Haitian Creole, a less-resourced language for which no POS-tagger is available.

4 Experimental Setup

We conducted experiments for two language pairs, English–German and Haitian Creole–English. We always applied the reordering rules to the translation input, creating a lattice of possible reorderings as input to the decoder. For the training data we applied two strategies. As the first option we used training data from the baseline system with original word order. As the second option we reordered the training data as well, using the learnt reordering rules to create reordering lattices for the training data, from which we

ID	Form	Lemma	Dependency	Functional tag	Syntax	POS	Morphology
1	Resumption	resumption	main:>0	@NH	%NH	N	NOM SG
2	of	of	mod:>1	@<NOM-OF	%N<	PREP	
3	the	the	attr:>4	@A>	%>N	DET	
4	session	session	pcomp:>2	@<P	%NH	N	NOM SG

Table 1: Parser output

extracted the 1-best reordering, as suggested by Rottmann and Vogel (2007).

For the supervised tagging of the English source side we use a commercial functional dependency parser.[1] The main reason for using a parser instead of a tagger was that we wanted to explore the effect of different tagging schemes, which was available from this parser. An example of a tagged English text can be seen in Table 1. In this work we used four types of tags extracted from the parser output, part-of-speech tags (pos), dependency tags (dep), functional tags (func) and shallow syntax tags (syntax). The dependency tags consist of the dependency label of the word and the POS-tag of its dependent. For the example in Table 1, the sequence of dependency tags is: `main_TOP mod_N attr_N pcomp_PREP`. The other tag types are directly exemplified in Table 1. The tagsets have different sizes, as shown in Table 2.

For the unsupervised tags, we used clustered word classes obtained using the mkcls software,[2] which implements the approach of Och (1999). We explored three different numbers of clusters, 50, 125, and 625. The clustering was performed on the same corpus as the SMT training.

The translation system used is a standard phrase-based SMT system. The translation model was trained by first creating unidirectional word alignments in both directions using GIZA++ (Och and Ney, 2003), which are then symmetrized by the grow-diag-final-and method (Koehn et al., 2005). From this many-to-many alignment, consistent phrases of up to length 7 were extracted. A 5-gram language model was used, produced by SRILM (Stolcke, 2002). For training and decoding we used the Moses toolkit (Koehn et al., 2007) and the feature weights were optimized using minimum error rate training (Och, 2003).

[1] `http://www.connexor.eu/technology/machinese/machinesesyntax/`

[2] `http://www-i6.informatik.rwth-aachen.de/web/Software/mkcls.html`

Tagset	Classes	Rules	Paths
pos	23	319147	2.1e09
dep	523	328415	2.8e09
func	49	325091	1.5e10
syntax	20	315407	4.5e11
class50	50	303292	6.2e09
class125	125	271348	1.3e07
class625	625	211606	31654

Table 2: Number of tags for each tagset in the English training corpus, number of rules extracted for each tagset, and average numbers of paths per sentence in the testset lattice using each tagset to create rules

The baseline systems were trained using no additional preordering, only a distance-based reordering penalty for modelling reordering. For the Haitian Creole–English experiments we also added a lexicalized reordering model (Koehn et al., 2005), both to the baseline and to the reordered systems.

For the English–German experiments, the translation system was trained and tested using a part of the Europarl corpus (Koehn, 2005). The training part contained 439513 sentences and 9.4 million words. Sentences longer than 40 words were filtered out. The test set has 2000 sentences and the development set has 500 sentences.

For the Haitian Creole–English experiments we used the SMS corpus released for WMT11 (Callison-Burch et al., 2011). The corpus contains 17192 sentences and 352326 words. The test and development data both contain 900 sentences each. Since we know of no POS-tagger for Haitian Creole, we only compare the clustered result to a baseline system.

Reordering rules were extracted from the same corpora that were used for training the SMT system. The word alignments needed for reordering were created using GIZA++ (Och and Ney, 2003), an implementation of the IBM models (Brown et al., 1993) of alignment, which is trained in a fully unsupervised manner based on the EM algorithm (Dempster et al., 1977).

5 Results

Table 2 shows the number of rules, and the average number of paths for each sentence in the test data lattice, using each tagset. For the standard tagsets the number of rules is relatively constant, despite the fact that the number of tags in the tagsets are quite different. For the clustered word classes, there are slightly fewer rules with 50 classes than for the standard tags, and the number of rules decreases with a higher number of classes. For the average number of lattice paths per sentence, there are some differences for the standard tags, but it is not related to tagset size. Again, the clustering with 50 classes has a similar number as the standard classes, but here there is a sharp decrease of lattice paths with a higher number of classes.

The translation results for the English–German experiments are shown in Table 3. We report translation results for two metrics, Bleu (Papineni et al., 2002) and NIST (Doddington, 2002), and significance testing is performed using approximate randomization (Riezler and Maxwell, 2005), with 10,000 iterations. All the systems with reordering have higher scores than the baseline on both metrics. This difference is always significant for NIST, and significant for Bleu in all cases except for two systems, one with standard tags and one with clustered tags. Between most of the systems with reordering the differences are small and most of them are not significant. Overall the systems with standard word classes perform slightly better than the clustered systems, especially the func tagset gives consistently high results, and is significantly better than four of the clustered systems on Bleu, and than one system on NIST. The fact that the number of paths were much smaller for a high number of clustered classes than for the other tagsets does not seem to have influenced the translation results.

Clustering of word classes is nondeterministic, and several runs of the cluster methods give different results, which could influence the translation results as well. To investigate this, we reran the experiment with 50 classes and baseline training data three times. The differences of the results between these runs were small, Bleu varied between 20.08–20.19 and NIST varied between 5.99–6.01. This variation is smaller than the difference between the baseline and the reordering systems, and should not influence the overall conclusions.

	Baseline training		Reordered training	
Tagset	Bleu	NIST	Bleu	NIST
Baseline	19.84	5.92	–	–
pos	20.34**	6.05**	20.26**	5.98*
dep	20.11	6.03**	20.25**	6.06**
func	20.40**	6.05**	20.40**	6.06**
syntax	20.29**	6.07**	20.32**	6.06**
class50	20.15*	6.05**	20.15*	5.99**
class125	20.15*	6.03**	20.17*	6.02**
class625	20.19**	6.05**	20.07	6.05**

Table 3: Translation results for English–German. Statistically significant differences from baseline scores are marked * ($p < 0.05$), ** ($p < 0.01$).

Tagset	Classes	Rules	Paths
class50	50	4588	3.70
class125	125	3554	1.46
class625	625	2388	1.42

Table 4: Number of classes for Haitian Creole, number of rules extracted for each tagset, and average numbers of paths per sentence in the testset lattice using each tagset to create rules

For the Haitian Creole testset both the average number of reorderings per sentence, and the number of rules, are substantially lower than for the English testset. As shown in Table 4, the trends are the same, however. With a higher number of classes there are both fewer rules and fewer rule applications. That there are few rules and paths can both depend on the fact that there are fewer word order differences between these languages, that the corpus is smaller, and that the sentence length is shorter.

Even though the number of reorderings is relatively small, there are consistent significant improvements for all reordered options on both Bleu and NIST compared to the baseline, as shown in Table 5. Between the clustered systems the differences are relatively small, and the only significant differences are that the system with 50 classes and reordered training data is worse on Bleu than 50 classes with baseline reordering and 125 classes with reordered training data, at the 0.05-level. The trend for the systems with 125 and 625 classes is in the other direction with slightly higher results with reordered data. There is hardly any difference between these two systems, which is not surprising, seeing that the number of ap-

	Baseline training		Reordered training	
Tagset	Bleu	NIST	Bleu	NIST
Baseline	29.04	5.58	–	–
class50	29.59**	5.73**	29.60**	5.69**
class125	29.52**	5.70**	29.78**	5.73**
class625	29.55**	5.70**	29.75**	5.74**

Table 5: Translation results for Haitian Creole–English. Statistically significant differences from baseline BLEU score are marked ** ($p < 0.01$).

plied rules is very similar.

6 Conclusion and Future Work

We have presented experiments of using clustered word classes as input to a preordering method for SMT. We showed that the proposed method perform better than a baseline and nearly on par with using standard tags for an English–German translation task. We also showed that it can improve results over a baseline when translating from the less-resourced language Haitian Creole into English, even though the word order differences between these languages are relatively small.

The suggested preordering algorithm with word classes is fully unsupervised, since unsupervised methods are used both for word classes and word alignments that are the basis of the preordering algorithm. This means that the method can be applied to less-resourced languages where no taggers or parsers are available, which is not the case for the many preordering methods which are based on POS-tags or parse trees.

This initial study is quite small, and in the future we plan to extend it to larger corpora and other language pairs. We would also like to compare the performance of different unsupervised word clustering and POS-tagging methods on this task.

Acknowledgments

I would like to thank Jan Niehues for sharing his code, and for his help on the POS-based reordering, and Joakim Nivre and the anonymous reviewers for their insightful comments.

References

Chris Biemann. 2006. Unsupervised part-of-speech tagging employing efficient graph clustering. In *Proceedings of the COLING/ACL 2006 Student Research Workshop*, pages 7–12, Sydney, Australia.

Peter F. Brown, Peter V. deSouza, Robert L. Mercer, Vincent J. Della Pietra, and Jenifer C. Lai. 1992. Class-based n-gram models of natural language. *Computational linguistics*, 18(4):467–479.

Peter F. Brown, Stephen Della Pietra, Vincent J. Della Pietra, and Robert L. Mercer. 1993. The mathematics of statistical machine translation: Parameter estimation. *Computational Linguistics*, 19(2):263–311.

Chris Callison-Burch, Philipp Koehn, Christof Monz, and Omar Zaidan. 2011. Findings of the 2011 workshop on statistical machine translation. In *Proceedings of WMT*, pages 22–64, Edinburgh, Scotland.

David Chiang. 2007. Hierarchical phrase-based translation. *Computational Linguistics*, 33(2):202–228.

Michael Collins, Philipp Koehn, and Ivona Kučerová. 2005. Clause restructuring for statistical machine translation. In *Proceedings of ACL*, pages 531–540, Ann Arbor, Michigan, USA.

Marta R. Costa-jussà and José A. R. Fonollosa. 2006. Statistical machine reordering. In *Proceedings of EMNLP*, pages 70–76, Sydney, Australia.

Marta R. Costa-jussà, Josep M. Crego, Patrik Lambert, Maxim Khalilov, José A. R. Fonollosa, José B. Mariño, and Rafael E. Banchs. 2007. Ngram-based statistical machine translation enhanced with multiple weighted reordering hypotheses. In *Proceedings of WMT*, pages 167–170, Prague, Czech Republic.

Arthur E. Dempster, Nan M. Laird, and Donald B. Rubin. 1977. Maximum likelihood from incomplete data via the EM algorithm. *Journal of the Royal Statistical Society*, 39(1):1–38.

George Doddington. 2002. Automatic evaluation of machine translation quality using n-gram cooccurence statistics. In *Proceedings of the Second International Conference on Human Language Technology*, pages 228–231, San Diego, California, USA.

Kevin Gimpel and Noah A. Smith. 2011. Generative models of monolingual and bilingual gappy patterns. In *Proceedings of WMT*, pages 512–522, Edinburgh, Scotland.

Sharon Goldwater and Tom Griffiths. 2007. A fully bayesian approach to unsupervised part-of-speech tagging. In *Proceedings of ACL*, pages 744–751, Prague, Czech Republic.

Nizar Habash. 2007. Syntactic preprocessing for statistical machine translation. In *Proceedings of MT Summit XI*, pages 215–222, Copenhagen, Denmark.

Dan Klein and Christopher Manning. 2004. Corpus-based induction of syntactic structure: Models of dependency and constituency. In *Proceedings of ACL*, pages 478–485, Barcelona, Spain.

Philipp Koehn, Amittai Axelrod, Alexandra Birch Mayne, Chris Callison-Burch, Miles Osborne, and

David Talbot. 2005. Edinburgh system description for the 2005 IWSLT speech translation evaluation. In *Proceedings of the International Workshop on Spoken Language Translation*, Pittsburgh, Pennsylvania, USA.

Philipp Koehn, Hieu Hoang, Alexandra Birch, Chris Callison-Burch, Marcello Federico, Nicola Bertoldi, Brooke Cowan, Wade Shen, Christine Moran, Richard Zens, Chris Dyer, Ondrej Bojar, Alexandra Constantin, and Evan Herbst. 2007. Moses: Open source toolkit for statistical machine translation. In *Proceedings of ACL, demonstration session*, pages 177–180, Prague, Czech Republic.

Philipp Koehn. 2005. Europarl: A parallel corpus for statistical machine translation. In *Proceedings of MT Summit X*, pages 79–86, Phuket, Thailand.

Terry Koo, Xavier Carreras, and Michael Collins. 2008. Simple semi-supervised dependency parsing. In *Proceedings of ACL*, pages 595–603, Columbus, Ohio.

Chi-Ho Li, Minghui Li, Dongdong Zhang, Mu Li, Ming Zhou, and Yi Guan. 2007. A probabilistic approach to syntax-based reordering for statistical machine translation. In *Proceedings of the 45th Annual Meeting of the ACL*, pages 720–727, Prague, Czech Republic.

Bernard Merialdo. 1994. Tagging English text with a probabilistic model. *Computational Linguistics*, 20(2):155–172.

Hwidong Na, Jin-Ji Li, Jungi Kim, and Jong-Hyeok Lee. 2009. Improving fluency by reordering target constituents using MST parser in English-to-Japanese phrase-based SMT. In *Proceedings of MT Summit XII*, pages 276–283, Ottawa, Ontario, Canada.

Jan Niehues and Muntsin Kolss. 2009. A POS-based model for long-range reorderings in SMT. In *Proceedings of WMT*, pages 206–214, Athens, Greece.

Jan Niehues, Teresa Herrmann, Muntsin Kolss, and Alex Waibel. 2009. The Universität Karlsruhe translation system for the EACL-WMT 2009. In *Proceedings of the Fourth Workshop on Statistical Machine Translation*, pages 80–84, Athens, Greece.

Franz Josef Och and Hermann Ney. 2003. A systematic comparison of various statistical alignment models. *Computational Linguistics*, 29(1):19–51.

Franz Josef Och. 1999. An efficient method for determining bilingual word classes. In *Proceedings of EACL*, pages 71–76, Bergen, Norway.

Franz Josef Och. 2003. Minimum error rate training in statistical machine translation. In *Proceedings of ACL*, pages 160–167, Sapporo, Japan.

Kishore Papineni, Salim Roukos, Todd Ward, and Wei-Jing Zhu. 2002. BLEU: A method for automatic evaluation of machine translation. In *Proceedings of ACL*, pages 311–318, Philadelphia, Pennsylvania, USA.

Maja Popović and Hermann Ney. 2006. POS-based reorderings for statistical machine translation. In *Proceedings of LREC*, pages 1278–1283, Genoa, Italy.

Stefan Riezler and John T. Maxwell. 2005. On some pitfalls in automatic evaluation and significance testing for MT. In *Proceedings of the Workshop on Intrinsic and Extrinsic Evaluation Measures for MT and/or Summarization at ACL'05*, pages 57–64, Ann Arbor, Michigan, USA.

Kay Rottmann and Stephan Vogel. 2007. Word reordering in statistical machine translation with a POS-based distortion model. In *Proceedings of the 11th International Conference on Theoretical and Methodological Issues in Machine Translation*, pages 171–180, Skövde, Sweden.

Hinrich Schütze. 1995. Distributional part-of-speech tagging. In *Proceedings of EACL*, pages 141–148, Dublin, Ireland.

Noah A. Smith and Jason Eisner. 2005. Contrastive estimation: Training log-linear models on unlabeled data. In *Proceedings of ACL*, pages 354–362, Ann Arbor, Michigan, USA.

Andreas Stolcke. 2002. SRILM – an extensible language modeling toolkit. In *Proceedings of ICSLP*, pages 901–904, Denver, Colorado, USA.

Fei Xia and Michael McCord. 2004. Improving a statistical MT system with automatically learned rewrite patterns. In *Proceedings of CoLing*, pages 508–514, Geneva, Switzerland.

Kenji Yamada and Kevin Knight. 2002. A decoder for syntax-based statistical MT. In *Proceedings of ACL*, pages 303–310, Philadelphia, Pennsylvania, USA.

Richard Zens and Hermann Ney. 2006. Discriminative reordering models for statistical machine translation. In *Proceedings of WMT*, pages 55–63, New York City, USA.

Yuqi Zhang, Richard Zens, and Hermann Ney. 2007. Improved chunk-level reordering for statistical machine translation. In *Proceedings of the International Workshop on Spoken Language Translation*, pages 21–28, Trento, Italy.

Improving Distantly Supervised Extraction of Drug-Drug and Protein-Protein Interactions

Tamara Bobić,[1,2*] **Roman Klinger,**[1*] **Philippe Thomas,**[3] **and Martin Hofmann-Apitius**[1,2]

[1]Fraunhofer Institute for Algorithms and Scientific Computing (SCAI)
Schloss Birlinghoven
53754 Sankt Augustin
Germany

[2]Bonn-Aachen Center for Information Technology
Dahlmannstraße 2
53113 Bonn
Germany

[3]Computer Science Institut
Humboldt-Universität
Unter den Linden 6
10099 Berlin
Germany

{tbobic,klinger,hofmann-apitius}@scai.fraunhofer.de
thomas@informatik.hu-berlin.de

Abstract

Relation extraction is frequently and successfully addressed by machine learning methods. The downside of this approach is the need for annotated training data, typically generated in tedious manual, cost intensive work. Distantly supervised approaches make use of weakly annotated data, like automatically annotated corpora.

Recent work in the biomedical domain has applied distant supervision for protein-protein interaction (PPI) with reasonable results making use of the IntAct database. Such data is typically noisy and heuristics to filter the data are commonly applied. We propose a constraint to increase the quality of data used for training based on the assumption that no self-interaction of real-world objects are described in sentences. In addition, we make use of the University of Kansas Proteomics Service (KUPS) database. These two steps show an increase of 7 percentage points (pp) for the PPI corpus AIMed. We demonstrate the broad applicability of our approach by using the same workflow for the analysis of drug-drug interactions, utilizing relationships available from the drug database DrugBank. We achieve 37.31 % in F_1 measure without manually annotated training data on an independent test set.

1 Introduction

Assuming co-mentioned entities to be related is an approach of extracting relations of real-world objects with limited precision. Extracting high quality interaction pairs from free text allows for building networks, *e. g.* of proteins, which need less manual curation to serve as a model for further knowledge processing steps. Nevertheless, just assuming co-occurrence to model an interaction or relation is common, as the development of interaction extraction systems can be time-consuming and complex.

Currently, a lot of relation extraction (RE) systems rely on machine learning, namely classifying pairs of entities to be related or not (Airola et al., 2008; Miwa et al., 2009; Kim et al., 2010). Despite the fact that machine learning has been most successful in identifying relevant relations in text, a drawback is the need for manually annotated training data. Domain experts have to dedicate time and effort to this tedious and labor-intensive process.

Specific biomedical domains have been explored more extensively than others, thus creating an imbalance in the number of existing corpora for a specific RE task. Protein-protein interactions (PPI) have been investigated the most, which gave rise to a number of available corpora. Pyysalo et al. (2008) standardized five PPI corpora to a unified XML format. Recently, a drug-drug-interaction (DDI) corpus is made available in the same format, originally for the DDI Extraction Workshop[1] (Segura-Bedmar et al., 2011b).

As a consequence of the overall scarcity of annotated corpora for RE in the biomedical domain, the approach of distant supervision, *e. g.* to automatically label a training set is emerging. Many approaches make use of the distant supervision assumption (Mintz et al., 2009; Riedel et al., 2010):

*These authors contributed equally.

[1]Associated with the conference of the spanish society for natural language processing (SEPLN) in 2011, http://labda.inf.uc3m.es/DDIExtraction2011/

If two entities participate in a relation, all sentences that mention these two entities express that relation.

Obviously, this assumption does not hold in general, and therefore exceptions need to be detected which are not used for training a model. Thomas et al. (2011b) successfully used simple filtering techniques in a distantly supervised setting to extract PPI. In contrast to their work, we introduce a more generic filter to detect frequent exceptions from the distant supervision assumption and make use of more data sources, by merging the interaction information from IntAct and KUPS databases (discussed in Section 2.1). In addition, we present the first system (to our knowledge), evaluating distant supervision for drug-drug interaction with promising results.

1.1 Related work

Distant supervision approaches have received considerable attention in the past few years. However, most of the work is focusing on domains other than biomedical texts.

Mintz et al. (2009) use distant supervision to learn to extract relations that are represented in Freebase (Bollacker et al., 2008). Yao et al. (2010) use Freebase as a source of supervision, dealing with entity identification and relation extraction in a joint fashion. Entity types are restricted to those compatible with selected relations. Riedel et al. (2010) argue that distant supervision leads to noisy training data that hurts precision and suggest a two step approach to reduce this problem. They identify the sentences which express the known relations ("expressed-at-least-once" assumption) and thus frame the problem of distant supervision as an instance of constraint-driven semi-supervision, achieving 31 % of error reduction.

Vlachos et al. (2009) tackle the problem of biomedical event extraction. The scope of their interest is to identify different event types without using a knowledge base as a source of supervision, but explore the possibility of inferring relations from the text based on the trigger words and dependency parsing, without previously annotated data.

Thomas et al. (2011b) develop a distantly labeled corpus for protein-protein interaction extraction. Different strategies are evaluated to select valuable training instances. Competitive results are obtained, compared to purely supervised methods.

Very recent work examines the usability of knowledge from PharmGKB (Gong et al., 2008) to generate training sets that capture gene-drug, gene-disease and drug-disease relations (Buyko et al., 2012). They evaluate the RE for the three interaction classes in intrisic and extrinsic experimental settings, reaching F_1 measure of around 80 % and up to 77.5 % respectively.

2 Resources

2.1 Interaction Databases

The IntAct database (Kerrien et al., 2012) contains protein-protein interaction information. It is freely available, manually curated and frequently updated. It consists of 290,947 binary interaction evidences, including 39,235 unique pairs of interacting proteins for human species.[2]

In general, PPI databases are underannotated and the overlap between them is marginal (De Las Rivas and Fontanillo, 2010). Combining several databases allows to cover a larger fraction of known interactions resulting in a more complete knowledge base. KUPS (Chen et al., 2010) is a database that combines entries from three manually curated PPI databases (IntAct, MINT (Chatr-aryamontri et al., 2007) and HPRD50 (Prasad et al., 2009)) and contains 185,446 positive pairs from various model organisms, out of which 69,600 belong to human species.[3] Enriching IntAct interaction information with the KUPS database leads to 57,589 unique pairs.[4]

The database DrugBank (Knox et al., 2011) combines detailed drug data with comprehensive drug target information. It consists of 6,707 drug entries. Apart from information about its targets, for certain drugs known interactions with other drugs are given. Altogether, we obtain 11,335 unique DDI pairs.

2.2 Corpora

For evaluation of protein-protein interaction, the five corpora made available by Pyysalo et al. (2008) are used. Their properties, like size and ratio of positive and negative examples, differ greatly,

[2]As of January 27th, 2012.

[3]As of August 16th, 2010.

[4]Only 45,684 out of 69,600 human PPI pairs are available from the KUPS web service due to computational and storage limitations (personal communication).

Corpus	Positive pairs	Negative pairs	Total
AIMed	1000 (0.17)	4,834 (0.82)	5,834
BioInfer	2,534 (0.26)	7,132 (0.73)	9,666
HPRD50	163 (0.38)	270 (0.62)	433
IEPA	335 (0.41)	482 (0.59)	817
LLL	164 (0.49)	166 (0.50)	330
DDI train	2,400 (0.10)	21,411 (0.90)	23,811
DDI test	755 (0.11)	6,275 (0.89)	7,030

Table 1: Basic statistics of the five PPI and two DDI corpora. Ratios are given in brackets.

the latter being the main cause of performance differences when evaluating on these corpora. Moreover, annotation guidelines and contexts differ: AIMed (Bunescu et al., 2005) and HPRD50 (Fundel et al., 2007) are human-focused, LLL (Nedellec, 2005) on Bacillus subtilis, BioInfer (Pyysalo et al., 2007) contains information from various organisms and IEPA (Ding et al., 2002) is made of sentences that describe 10 selected chemicals, the majority of which are proteins, and their interactions.

For the purposes of DDI extraction, the corpus published by Segura-Bedmar et al. (2011b) is used. This corpus is generated from web-documents describing drug effects. It is divided into a training and testing set. An overview of the corpora is given in Table 1.

3 Methods

In this section, the relation extraction system used for classification of interacting pairs is presented. Furthermore, the process of generating an automatically labeled corpus is explained in more detail, along with specific characteristics of the PPI and DDI task.

3.1 Interaction Classification

We formulate the task of relation extraction as feature-based classification of co-occurring entities in a sentence. Those are assigned to be either related or not, without identifying the type of relation. Our RE system is based on rich feature vectors and the linear support vector machine classifier LibLINEAR, which has shown high performance (in runtime as well as model accuracy) on large and sparse data sets (Fan et al., 2008).

The approach is based on lexical features, optionally with dependency parsing features created using the Stanford parser (Marneffe et al., 2006). Lexical features are bag-of-words (BOW) and n-

Methods	P	R	F_1
Thomas et al. (2011a)	60.54	**71.92**	**65.74**
Chowdhury et al. (2011)	58.59	70.46	63.98
Chowdhury and Lavelli (2011)	58.39	70.07	63.70
Björne et al. (2011)	58.04	68.87	62.99
Minard et al. (2011)	55.18	64.90	59.65
Our system (*lex*)	63.30	52.32	57.28
Our system (*lex+dep*)	**66.46**	56.69	61.19

Table 2: Comparison of fully supervised relations extraction systems for DDI. (*lex* denotes the use of lexical features, *lex+dep* the additional use of dependency parsing-based features.)

grams based, with $n \in \{1, 2, 3, 4\}$. They encompass the local (window size 3) and global (window size 13) context left and right of the entity pair, along with the area between the entities (Li et al., 2010). Additionally, dictionary based domain specific trigger words are taken into account.

The respective dependency parse tree is included through following the shortest dependency path hypothesis (Bunescu and Mooney, 2005), by using the syntactical and dependency information of edges (*e*) and vertices (*v*). So-called *v-walks* and *e-walks* of length 3 are created as well as n grams along the shortest path (Miwa et al., 2010).

3.2 Automatically Labeling a Corpus in General

One of the most important source of publications in the biomedical domain is MEDLINE[5], currently containing more than 21 million citations.[6] The initial step is annotation of named entities – in our case performed by ProMiner (Hanisch et al., 2005), a tool proving state-of-the-art results in *e. g.* the BioCreative competition (Fluck et al., 2007). Based on the named entity recognition, only sentences containing co-occurrences are further processed. Based on the distant supervision assumption, each pair of entities is labeled as related if mentioned so in a structured interaction databases. Note that this requires the step of entity normalization.

3.3 Filtering Noise

A sentence may contain two entities of an interacting pair (as known from a database), but does not describe their interaction. Likewise, a sentence

[5] http://www.ncbi.nlm.nih.gov/pubmed/
[6] As of January, 2012.

may talk about a novel interaction which has not been stored in the database. Therefore, filtering strategies need to be employed to help in deciding which pairs are annotated as being related and which not.

Thomas et al. (2011b) propose the use of trigger words, *i. e.*, an entity pair of a certain sentence is marked as *positive* (related) if the database has information about their interaction and the sentence contains at least one trigger word. Similarly, a *negative* (non-related) example is a pair of entities that does not interact according to the database and their sentence does not contain any trigger word. Pairs which do not fulfil both constraints are discarded.

Towards improvement of the heuristics for reducing noise, we introduce the constraint of "auto-interaction filtering" (AIF): If entities from an entity pair both refer to the same real-world object, the pair is labeled as not interacting. Even though self-interactions are known for proteins and drugs, such pairs can rarely be observed to describe an interaction but rather are repeated occurences or abbreviations. Moreover, the fundamental advantage of AIF is that it requires no additional manual effort.

3.4 Application on Protein-Protein Interaction and Drug-Drug Interaction

In biomedical texts there are often mentions of multiple proteins in the same sentence. However, this co-occurrence does not necessarily signal that the sentence is talking about their relation. Hence, to reduce noise, a list of trigger words specific to the problem is required. The rationale behind this filter is that the interaction between two entities is usually expressed by a specific (trigger) word. For protein-protein-interactions, we use the trigger list compiled by Thomas et al. (2011b)[7]. In addition to using IntAct alone, we introduce the use of KUPS database (as described in Section 2.2).

For drug-drug-interaction, to our knowledge, no DDI-specific trigger word list developed by domain experts is available. Therefore, filtering via such term occurrences is not applied in this case.

[7] http://www2.informatik.hu-berlin.de/~thomas/pub/2011/iwords.txt

4 Results

In this section, we start with an overview of state-of-the-art results for fully supervised relation extraction on PPI and DDI corpora (see Table 1). Furthermore, experimental settings for distant supervision are explained. Finally, we present specific results for models trained on distantly labeled data, when evaluated on manually annotated PPI and DDI corpora.

4.1 Performance overview of supervised RE systems

Protein-protein interactions has been extensively investigated in the past decade because of their biological significance. Machine learning approaches have shown the best performance in this domain (*e. g.* BioNLP (Cohen et al., 2011) and DDIExtraction Shared Task (Segura-Bedmar et al., 2011a)). Table 3 gives a comparison of RE systems' performances on 5 PPI corpora, determined by document level 10-fold cross-validation.[8] The use of dependency parsing-based features increases the F_1 measure by almost 4 pp.

Table 2 shows results of the five best performing systems on the held out test data set of the DDI extraction workshop (Segura-Bedmar et al., 2011b). In addition, the result of our system is shown. Note that the first three systems use ensemble based methods combining the output of several different systems.

The results presented in Table 2 and 3 give a performance overview of the RE system used in distant learning strategies.

4.2 Experimental Setting

To avoid information leakage and biased classification, all documents which are contained in the test corpus are removed. For each experiment we sample random subsets to reduce processing time. This allows us to evaluate the impact of different combinations of subset size and the ratio of related and non-related (pos/neg) entity pairs, having in mind the problem of imbalanced datasets (Chawla et al., 2004). All experiments are performed five times to reduce the influence of sampling different subsets. This leads to more reliable precision, recall, and F_1 values.

[8] Separating into training and validation sets is performed on document level, not on instance (entity pair) level. The latter could lead to an unrealisticallly optimistic estimate (Van Landeghem et al., 2008)

	AIMed			BioInfer			HPRD50			IEPA			LLL		
	P	R	F_1	P	R	F_1	P	R	F_1	P	R	F_1	P	R	F_1
(Airola et al., 2008)	52.9	61.8	56.4	56.7	67.2	61.3	64.3	65.8	63.4	69.6	**82.7**	**75.1**	72.5	87.2	76.8
(Kim et al., 2010)	61.4	53.2	56.6	61.8	54.2	57.6	66.7	69.2	67.8	**73.7**	71.8	72.9	76.9	**91.1**	**82.4**
(Fayruzov et al., 2009)			39.0			34.0			56.0			72.0			76.0
(Liu et al., 2010)			54.7			59.8			64.9			62.1			78.1
(Miwa et al., 2009)	55.0	**68.8**	**60.8**	**65.7**	**71.1**	**68.1**	68.5	**76.1**	**70.9**	67.5	78.6	71.7	**77.6**	86.0	80.1
(Tikk et al., 2010)	47.5	65.5	54.5	55.1	66.5	60.0	64.4	67	64.2	71.2	69.3	69.3	74.5	85.3	74.5
Our s. (*lex*)	62.3	46.3	53.1	59.1	54.3	56.6	**69.7**	69.4	69.6	67.5	73.2	70.2	66.9	84.6	74.7
Our s. (*lex+dep*)	**65.1**	48.6	55.7	64.7	57.6	61.0	69.3	69.8	69.5	67.0	72.5	69.7	71.2	86.3	78.0

Table 3: Comparison of fully supervised relations extraction systems for PPI.

Strategy	Pairs	Positive pairs	Sentences
1	3,304,033	511,665 (0.155)	842,339
2	5,560,975	1,389,036 (0.250)	1,172,920
3	2,764,626	359,437 (0.130)	780,658
4	3,454,805	650,455 (0.188)	896,344

Table 4: Statistics of the fours strategies used in distant supervision for PPI task: 1) IntAct, 2) IntAct + KUPS, 3) IntAct + AIF, 4) IntAct + KUPS + AIF. Ratios are given in brackets.

4.3 Protein-protein interaction

We explore four strategies to determine the impact of using additional database knowledge (IntAct and KUPS) and to test the utility of our novel condition (AIF).

Table 4 shows the difference in retrieved number of sentences and protein pairs, including the percentage of positive examples in the whole data set. As expected, by using more background knowledge, the number of sentences and instances retrieved from MEDLINE rises. An increase of both negative and positive pairs is observed, since a relevant sentence can have negative pairs along with the positive ones. After applying additional interaction knowledge, the fraction of positive examples (see 3rd column in Table 4) increases from 15.5 % (IntAct) to 25 % (IntAct+KUPS). However, employment of the AIF condition to both IntAct and IntAct+KUPS strategies leads to a reduction of these values (*e. g.* fraction of positive examples reduces from 15.5 % to 13 % and from 25 % to 18.8 %).

For simplicity reasons all runs are performed using only lexical features.

Table 5 shows the average values of distant supervision experiments carried out for the PPI task. A significant correlation between pos/neg ratio and precision/recall holds. This clearly indicates the tendency of classifiers to assign more test instances to the class more often observed during training. In accordance with their class distribution, AIMed reaches highest performance in case of lower fraction of positive instances (*i. e.* 30 % or 40 %), while for IEPA and LLL the optimal ratio is in favor of the positive class (*i. e.* 70 % or 80 %).

Comparative results of the distant learning strategies IntAct and IntAct+KUPS tested on five PPI corpora indicate that additional knowledge bases do not help per se. Supplementary employment of the KUPS database leads to a drop in performances seen in four out of five test cases (a decrease of 1.7 pp in F_1 measure is most notably observed in case of HPRD50). However, introduction of the novel filtering condition, in both strategies IntAct+AIF and IntAct+KUPS+AIF, shows a favorable effect on the precision and leads to an increase of up to 6 pp in F_1 measure, compared to IntAct and IntAct+KUPS.

Applying AIF to the baseline IntAct increases F_1 measure of AIMed and HPRD50 from 34.4 % to 37.8 % and from 56.1 % to 59.1 %, respectively. An even larger impact is observed when comparing IntAct+KUPS and IntAct+KUPS+AIF. For AIMed, HPRD50 and IEPA an increase of around 6 pp is achieved, while F_1 measure of BioInfer and LLL is improved around 3 pp. Table 5 clearly shows that IntAct+KUPS+AIF is outperforming other strategies in all five test cases by achieving F_1 measures of 39.0 % for AIMed, 52.0 % for BioInfer, 60.2 % for HPRD50, 63.4 % for IEPA and 69.3 % for LLL.

Analysis of the database (IntAct+KUPS) pairs reveals that in total there are 5,550 (around 10 %) proteins that interact with themselves, with 4,918 (89 %) originating from the KUPS database. This indicates a number of instances that represent auto-interacting proteins which contribute to increase of false positives. Such proportion where a majority of them come from KUPS explains the decrease

Strategy	pos/neg	AIMed			BioInfer			HPRD50			IEPA			LLL		
		P	R	F_1	P	R	F_1	P	R	F_1	P	R	F_1	P	R	F_1
IntAct	30-70	22.3	75.8	**34.4**	41.7	54.1	46.9	42.6	73.8	53.9	44.6	70.3	54.5	58.9	63.5	61.0
	40-60	21.5	83.5	34.2	40.0	61.9	48.5	42.0	81.7	55.5	44.4	78.0	56.6	55.7	73.3	63.2
	50-50	20.8	87.0	33.5	38.7	67.1	49.0	41.4	86.9	**56.1**	43.7	82.2	57.1	54.6	80.7	65.1
	60-40	20.0	90.8	32.8	37.3	72.6	**49.2**	40.5	91.2	**56.1**	43.2	85.6	57.4	52.4	86.7	65.3
	70-30	19.0	94.5	32.1	35.4	79.5	48.9	39.6	93.4	55.6	42.6	89.3	57.7	50.7	92.1	**65.4**
	80-20	18.6	96.8	31.2	33.5	86.5	48.3	38.6	96.2	55.1	42.1	93.3	**58.1**	49.4	96.7	65.0
IntAct + KUPS	30-70	20.6	48.9	29.0	37.5	30.0	33.3	38.6	45.8	41.8	33.1	25.3	28.6	55.3	25.4	34.6
	40-60	21.6	70.3	33.0	39.3	47.4	42.9	40.7	70.2	51.5	41.0	49.6	44.9	58.6	49.3	53.2
	50-50	20.8	81.6	**33.2**	38.2	59.4	46.5	39.6	80.4	53.0	42.9	65.3	51.8	58.5	61.1	59.5
	60-40	20.0	89.0	32.7	37.0	68.8	48.2	38.9	87.4	53.8	43.4	76.8	55.4	55.2	74.4	63.2
	70-30	19.2	94.3	31.9	35.2	79.1	**48.7**	38.6	92.3	**54.4**	42.9	86.2	57.2	52.8	88.5	66.1
	80-20	18.3	97.5	30.9	32.2	88.6	47.3	37.8	96.1	54.2	41.9	92.7	**57.8**	50.8	97.0	**66.6**
IntAct + AIF	30-70	25.1	76.7	**37.8**	42.8	54.1	47.7	45.7	75.7	57.0	49.9	77.2	60.6	58.4	69.5	63.4
	40-60	24.5	78.9	37.4	42.3	56.5	48.3	46.1	79.2	58.3	49.2	79.0	60.7	58.2	72.8	64.6
	50-50	23.9	81.1	36.9	42.3	59.2	49.2	45.9	83.1	**59.1**	49	81.6	61.2	57.8	75.5	65.3
	60-40	23.1	83.8	36.1	41.8	63.3	50.3	44.9	85.3	58.8	48.4	84.7	61.6	56.8	79.2	66.1
	70-30	22.1	85.8	35.2	40.8	66.4	**50.5**	43.9	86.5	58.2	47.6	87.9	**61.8**	56.3	82.1	**66.7**
	80-20	21.3	88.3	34.3	39.6	69.9	**50.5**	42.9	89.8	58.1	46.0	91.6	61.3	54.0	84.9	66.0
IntAct + KUPS + AIF	30-70	26.6	72.1	38.8	43.8	50.8	47.0	48.1	78.6	59.7	51.1	75.3	60.9	60.2	63.7	61.8
	40-60	26.0	77.8	**39.0**	43.2	55.4	48.5	47.6	82.5	60.4	50.7	80.6	62.2	58.8	68.7	63.3
	50-50	25.5	81.6	38.8	44.8	56.2	49.8	46.0	83.9	59.4	51.4	78.7	62.2	60.3	72.2	65.6
	60-40	24.6	84.1	38.0	44.5	60.0	51.1	45.6	88.6	**60.2**	50.6	83.8	63.1	59.4	77.8	67.3
	70-30	23.6	86.7	37.1	43.3	64.4	51.8	44.3	90.5	59.5	49.3	88.8	**63.4**	59.4	83.3	**69.3**
	80-20	22.1	90.4	35.5	41.0	71.3	**52.0**	42.5	93.4	58.4	46.8	91.8	62.0	56.2	88.2	68.6
Thomas et al. (2011b)		22.3	81.3	35.0	38.7	76.0	51.2	45.6	92.9	61.2	42.6	88.3	57.3	53.7	93.3	68.1
Tikk et al. (2010)		28.3	86.6	42.6	62.8	36.5	46.2	56.9	68.7	62.2	71.0	52.5	60.4	79.0	57.3	66.4
Our system		34.3	74.0	46.9	70.8	22.5	34.2	63.3	61.3	62.3	70.0	46.0	55.5	82.4	45.7	58.8
Co-occurrence		17.1	100	29.3	26.2	100	41.5	37.6	100	54.7	41.0	100	58.2	49.7	100	66.4

Table 5: Results achieved with lexical features, trained on 10,000 distantly labeled instances and tested on 5 PPI corpora.

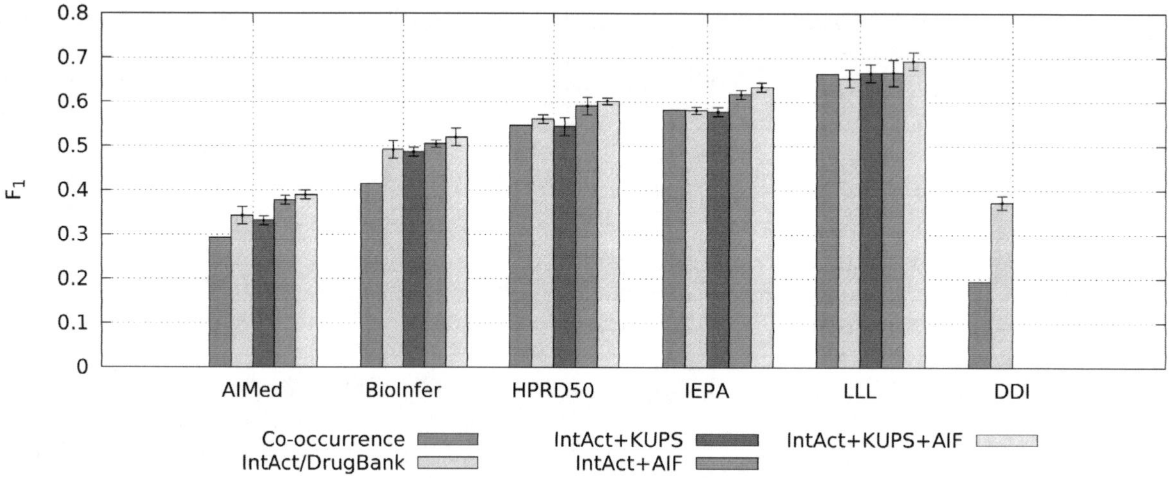

Figure 1: Comparison of four distant learning strategies with co-occurrence baseline. “IntAct/DrugBank” denotes the database used as source of supervision for PPI corpora and DDI corpus, respectively.

of performance in strategy IntAct+KUPS and the recovery after applying the AIF condition.

The strategy IntAct+KUPS+AIF results in a higher quality of data used for training and achieves the best performance in all five test cases thus proving the effectiveness of the novel condition. More knowledge is beneficial, but only when appropriate filtering of the data is applied.

Distantly supervised systems outperform co-occurrence results for all five PPI corpora. Considering the best performing strategy (IntAct+KUPS+AIF), F_1 measure of AIMed and BioInfer, for which we assume to have the most realistic pos/neg ratio, increased around 10 pp. HPRD50, IEPA and LLL have an improvement of 5.5 pp, 5.2 pp and 2.9 pp respectively, due to high fractions of positive instances (leading to a strong co-occurrence baseline).

Cross-learning[9] evaluation may be more realistic to be compared to distant-learning than cross validation (Airola et al., 2008). For AIMed and HPRD50 our approach performs on a par with Tikk et al. (2010) or better (up to 6 pp for BioInfer).

4.4 Drug-drug interaction

The problem of drug-drug interactions has not been previously explored in terms of distant supervision. It is noteworthy that DDI corpora are generated from web documents discussing drug effects which are in general not contained in MEDLINE. Hence, this evaluation corpus can be considered as out-domain and provides additional insights on the robustness of distant-supervision. The AIF setting is not evaluated for the DDI task, because only 1 of all 11,335 unique pairs describes a self interaction. In MEDLINE, only 7 sentences with multiple mentions of this drug (Sulfathiazole, DrugBank identifier DB06147) are found.

Table 6 gives an overview of the results for distant supervision on DDI, with the parameter of size of the training corpus and the pos/neg ratio. A slight increase in F_1 measure can be observed with additional training instances, both in case of using just lexical features and when dependency based features are additionally utilized (*e. g.* *(lex+dep)* from 36.2 % (5k) to 37.3 % (25k) in F_1 measure).

Accounting for dependency parsing features leads to an increase of 0.5 pp in F_1 measure, *i. e.* from 36.5 % to 37.0 % (10k) and 36.7% to 37.3 % (25k)), the latter being our best result obtained for weakly supervised DDI.

[9]For five PPI corpora: train on four, test on the remaining.

size	pos/neg	P	R	F_1
5k	30-70	**35.4**	32.4	33.7
	40-60	33.3	37.0	34.9
	50-50	31.9	41.7	36.0
	50-50 (lex+dep)	32.7	40.7	**36.2**
	60-40	30.1	46.6	**36.5**
	70-30	27.4	**51.8**	35.7
10k	30-70	**36.0**	34.4	34.9
	40-60	34.2	38.9	36.3
	50-50	32.9	41.0	**36.5**
	50-50 (lex+dep)	33.8	41.1	**37.0**
	60-40	30.8	44.8	36.4
	70-30	28.2	**48.7**	35.6
25k	30-70	**35.8**	35.0	35.3
	40-60	34.3	38.6	36.2
	50-50	33.2	41.1	**36.7**
	50-50 (lex+dep)	32.5	43.7	**37.3**
	60-40	31.7	42.6	36.3
	70-30	28.9	**47.2**	35.7
Co-occurrence		10.7	100	19.4

Table 6: Results for distant supervision with only lexical features on the DDI test corpus.

Compared to co-occurence, a gain of around 18 pp is achieved. Taking into account the high class imbalance of the DDI test set (see Table 1), which is most similar to AIMed corpus, the F_1 measure of 37.3 % is encouraging.

Figure 1 shows the results of PPI and DDI experiments in addition. The error bars denote the standard deviation over 5 differently sampled training corpora.

5 Discussion

This paper presents the application of distant supervision on the task to find protein-protein interactions and drug-drug interactions. The first is addressed using the databases IntAct and KUPS, the second using DrugBank.

More database knowledge does not necessarily have a positive impact on a trained model, appropriate instance selection methods need to be applied. This is demonstrated with the KUPS database and the automatic curation via auto-interaction filtering leading to state-of-the-art results for weakly supervised protein-protein interaction detection.

We present the first results of applying the distant supervision paradigm to drug-drug-interaction.

The results may seem comparatively limited in comparison to protein-protein interaction, but are encouraging when taking into account the imbalance of the test corpus and its differing source domain.

Future development of noise reduction approaches is important to make use of the full potential of available database knowledge. The results shown are encouraging that manual annotation of corpora can be avoided in other application areas as well. Another future direction is the investigation of specifically difficult structures, *e. g.* listings and enumerations of entities in a sentence.

Acknowledgments

We would like to thank the reviewers for their valuable feedback. Thanks to Sumit Madan and Theo Mevissen for fruitful discussions. T. Bobić was partially funded by the Bonn-Aachen International Center for Information Technology (B-IT) Research School. P. Thomas was funded by the German Federal Ministry of Education and Research (grant No 0315417B). R. Klinger was partially funded by the European Community's Seventh Framework Programme [FP7/2007-2011] under grant agreement no. 248726. We acknowledge financial support provided by the IMI-JU, grant agreement no. 115191 (Open PHACTS).

References

A. Airola, S. Pyysalo, J. Björne, T. Pahikkala, F. Ginter, and T. Salakoski. 2008. All-paths Graph Kernel for Protein-protein Interaction Extraction with Evaluation of Cross-corpus Learning. *BMC Bioinformatics*, 9(Suppl 11):S2.

J. Björne, A. Airola, T. Pahikkala, and T. Salakoski. 2011. Drug-drug interaction extraction with RLS and SVM classiffers. In *Challenge Task on Drug-Drug Interaction Extraction*, pages 35–42.

K. Bollacker, C. Evans, P. Paritosh, T. Sturge, and J. Taylor. 2008. Freebase: a collaboratively created graph database for structuring human knowledge. In *SIGMOD*.

R. C. Bunescu and R. J. Mooney. 2005. A shortest path dependency kernel for relation extraction. In *HLT and EMNLP*.

R. C. Bunescu, R. Ge, R. J. Kate, E. M. Marcotte, R. J. Mooney, A. K. Ramani, and Y. Wah Wong. 2005. Comparative experiments on learning information extractors for proteins and their interactions. *Artif Intell Med*, 33(2):139–155, Feb.

E. Buyko, E. Beisswanger, and U. Hahn. 2012. The extraction of pharmacogenetic and pharmacogenomic relations–a case study using pharmgkb. *PSB*, pages 376–387.

A. Chatr-aryamontri, A. Ceol, L. M. Palazzi, G. Nardelli, M.V. Schneider, L. Castagnoli, and G. Cesareni. 2007. MINT: the Molecular INTeraction database. *Nucleic Acids Res*, 35(Database issue):D572–D574.

N. V. Chawla, N Japkowicz, and A. Kotcz. 2004. Editorial: special issue on learning from imbalanced data sets. *SIGKDD Explor. Newsl.*, 6:1–6.

X. Chen, J. C. Jeong, and P. Dermyer. 2010. KUPS: constructing datasets of interacting and non-interacting protein pairs with associated attributions. *Nucleic Acids Res*, 39(Database issue):D750–D754.

F. M. Chowdhury and A. Lavelli. 2011. Drug-drug interaction extraction using composite kernels. In *Challenge Task on Drug-Drug Interaction Extraction*, pages 27–33.

F. M. Chowdhury, A. B. Abacha, A. Lavelli, and P. Zweigenbaum. 2011. Two different machine learning techniques for drug-drug interaction extraction. In *Challenge Task on Drug-Drug Interaction Extraction*, pages 19–26.

K. B. Cohen, D. Demner-Fushman, S. Ananiadou, J. Pestian, J. Tsujii, and B. Webber, editors. 2011. *Proceedings of the BioNLP*.

J. De Las Rivas and C. Fontanillo. 2010. Protein-protein interactions essentials: key concepts to building and analyzing interactome networks. *PLoS Comput Biol*, 6:e1000807+.

J. Ding, D. Berleant, D. Nettleton, and E. Wurtele. 2002. Mining MEDLINE: abstracts, sentences, or phrases? *Pac Symp Biocomput*, pages 326–337.

E. Fan, K. Chang, C. Hsieh, X. Wang, and C. Lin. 2008. LIBLINEAR: A Library for Large Linear Classification. *Machine Learning Research*, 9:1871–1874.

T. Fayruzov, M. De Cock, C. Cornelis, and V. Hoste. 2009. Linguistic feature analysis for protein interaction extraction. *BMC Bioinformatics*, 10(1):374.

J. Fluck, H. T. Mevissen, H. Dach, M. Oster, and M. Hofmann-Apitius. 2007. ProMiner: Recognition of Human Gene and Protein Names using regularly updated Dictionaries. In *BioCreative 2*, pages 149–151.

K. Fundel, R. Kuffner, and R. Zimmer. 2007. Relex-relation extraction using dependency parse trees. *Bioinformatics*, 23(3):365–371.

L. Gong, R. P. Owen, W. Gor, R. B. Altman, and T. E. Klein. 2008. PharmGKB: an integrated resource of pharmacogenomic data and knowledge. *Curr Protoc Bioinformatics*, Chapter 14:Unit14.7.

D. Hanisch, K. Fundel, H. T. Mevissen, R. Zimmer, and J. Fluck. 2005. ProMiner: rule-based protein and gene entity recognition. *BMC Bioinformatics*, 6(Suppl 1):S14.

S. Kerrien, B. Aranda, L. Breuza, A. Bridge, F. Broackes-Carter, C. Chen, M. Duesbury, M. Dumousseau, M. Feuermann, U. Hinz, C. Jandrasits, R.C. Jimenez, J. Khadake, U. Mahadevan, P. Masson, I. Pedruzzi, E. Pfeiffenberger, P. Porras, A. Raghunath, B. Roechert, S. Orchard, and H. Hermjakob. 2012. The IntAct molecular interaction database in 2012. *Nucleic Acids Res*, 40:D841–D846.

S. Kim, J. Yoon, J. Yang, and S. Park. 2010. Walk-weighted subsequence kernels for protein-protein interaction extraction. *BMC Bioinformatics*, 11:107.

C. Knox, V. Law, T. Jewison, P. Liu, S. Ly, A. Frolkis, A. Pon, K. Banco, C. Mak, V. Neveu, Y. Djoumbou, R. Eisner, A. Chi Guo, and D.S Wishart. 2011. Drugbank 3.0: a comprehensive resource for 'omics' research on drugs. *Nucleic Acids Res*, 39(Database issue):D1035–D1041.

Y. Li, X. Hu, H. Lin, and Z. Yang. 2010. Learning an enriched representation from unlabeled data for protein-protein interaction extraction. *BMC Bioinformatics*, 11(Suppl 2):S7.

B. Liu, L. Qian, H. Wang, and G. Zhou. 2010. Dependency-driven feature-based learning for extracting protein-protein interactions from biomedical text. In *COLING*, pages 757–765.

M. C. De Marneffe, B. Maccartney, and C. D. Manning. 2006. Generating typed dependency parses from phrase structure parses. In *LREC*.

A. L. Minard, L. Makour, A. L. Ligozat, and B. Grau. 2011. Feature Selection for Drug-Drug Interaction Detection Using Machine-Learning Based Approaches. In *Challenge Task on Drug-Drug Interaction Extraction*, pages 43–50.

M. Mintz, S. Bills, R. Snow, and D. Jurafsky. 2009. Distant supervision for relation extraction without labeled data. In *ACL-IJCNLP*, pages 1003–1011.

M. Miwa, R. Saetre, Y. Miyao, and J. Tsujii. 2009. A Rich Feature Vector for Protein-Protein Interaction Extraction from Multiple Corpora. *EMNLP*, 1(1):121–130.

M. Miwa, R. Saetre, J. D. Kim, and J. Tsujii. 2010. Event extraction with complex event classification using rich features. *J Bioinform Comput Biol*, 8(1):131–146.

C. Nedellec. 2005. Learning language in logic-genic interaction extraction challenge. In *Proc. of the ICML05 workshop: Learning Language in Logic (LLL'05)*, volume 18, pages 97–99.

T. S. Prasad, R. Goel, K. Kandasamy, S. Keerthikumar, S. Kumar, S. Mathivanan, D. Telikicherla, R. Raju, B. Shafreen, A. Venugopal, L. Balakrishnan, A. Marimuthu, S. Banerjee, D. S. Somanathan, A. Sebastian, S. Rani, S. Ray, C. J. Kishore, S. Kanth, M. Ahmed, M. K. Kashyap, R. Mohmood, Y. L. Ramachandra, V. Krishna, B. A.Rahiman, S. Mohan, P. Ranganathan, S. Ramabadran, R. Chaerkady, and A. Pandey. 2009. Human Protein Reference Database–2009 update. *Nucleic Acids Res*, 37(Database issue):D767–D772.

S. Pyysalo, F. Ginter, J. Heimonen, J. Björne, J. Boberg, J. Järvinen, and T. Salakoski. 2007. Bioinfer: A corpus for information extraction in the biomedical domain. *BMC Bioinformatics*, 8(50).

S. Pyysalo, A. Airola, J. Heimonen, J. Björne, F. Ginter, and T. Salakoski. 2008. Comparative analysis of five protein–protein interaction corpora. *BMC Bioinformatics*, 9 Suppl 3:S6.

S. Riedel, L. Yao, and A. McCallum. 2010. Modeling Relations and Their Mentions without Labeled Text. In *ECML PKDD*.

I. Segura-Bedmar, P. Martínez, and D. Sanchez-Cisneros, editors. 2011a. *Proceedings of the 1st Challenge Task on Drug-Drug Interaction Extraction*.

I. Segura-Bedmar, P. Martínez, and D. Sanchez-Cisneros. 2011b. The 1st DDIExtraction-2011 challenge task: Extraction of Drug-Drug Interactions from biomedical texts. In *Challenge Task on Drug-Drug Interaction Extraction 2011*, pages 1–9.

P. Thomas, M. Neves, I. Solt, D. Tikk, and U. Leser. 2011a. Relation Extraction for Drug-Drug Interactions using Ensemble Learning. In *Challenge Task on Drug-Drug Interaction Extraction*, pages 11–18.

P. Thomas, I. Solt, R. Klinger, and U. Leser. 2011b. Learning Protein Protein Interaction Extraction using Distant Supervision. In *Robust Unsupervised and Semi-Supervised Methods in Natural Language Processing*, pages 34–41.

D. Tikk, P. Thomas, P. Palaga, J. Hakenberg, and U. Leser. 2010. A comprehensive benchmark of kernel methods to extract protein-protein interactions from literature. *PLoS Comput Biol*, 6:e1000837.

S. Van Landeghem, Y. Saeys, B. De Baets, and Y. Van de Peer. 2008. Extracting protein-protein interactions from text using rich feature vectors and feature selection. *SMBM*, pages 77–84.

A. Vlachos, P. Buttery, D. Ó Séaghdha, and T. Briscoe. 2009. Biomedical Event Extraction without Training Data. In *BioNLP*, pages 37–40.

L. Yao, S. Riedel, and A. McCallum. 2010. Collective Cross-Document Relation Extraction Without Labeled Data. In *EMNLP*.

Robust Induction of Parts-of-Speech in Child-Directed Language by Co-Clustering of Words and Contexts

Richard E. Leibbrandt
School of Computer Science, Engineering and Mathematics
Flinders University

richard.leibbrandt@flinders.edu.au

David M W Powers
School of Computer Science, Engineering and Mathematics
Flinders University

david.powers@flinders.edu.au

Abstract

We introduce Conflict-Driven Co-Clustering, a novel algorithm for data co-clustering, and apply it to the problem of inducing parts-of-speech in a corpus of child-directed spoken English. Co-clustering is preferable to unidimensional clustering as it takes into account both item and context ambiguity. We show that the categorization performance of the algorithm is comparable with the co-clustering algorithm of Leibbrandt and Powers (2008), but out-performs that algorithm in robustly pruning less-useful clusters and merging them into categories strongly corresponding to the three main open classes of English.

1 Introduction

The problem of unsupervised part-of-speech induction has received considerable attention in computational linguistics (for a recent comparison of several influential models, see Christodoulopoulos, Goldwater & Steedman, 2010). A common approach is to estimate the parameters of a generative model given the natural language data, with the model usually a variant of a Hidden Markov Model (e.g. Goldwater & Griffiths, 2007; Berg-Kirkpatrick, Côté, De Nero & Klein, 2010; Moon, Erk & Baldridge, 2010). These models are often evaluated on corpora of formal, written English, such as the Penn Treebank, rather than on natural, spoken language, and typically the aim of these studies is to improve the state-of-the-art of POS induction using various techniques from machine learning, with an implicit focus on devising techniques that can be used in practical applications.

In the current paper, on the other hand, our focus is on part-of-speech induction mechanisms that children might use when learning their first language. Hence, we are interested in models that are motivated by psychological considerations, rather than by a more abstract mathematical or statistical grounding. In language acquisition research, a typical approach to part-of-speech induction is to make use of clustering. We will review this work and argue for the particular utility of two-mode clustering or co-clustering approaches, before presenting two novel co-clustering techniques and evaluating their performance in part-of-speech tagging on a corpus of child-directed English.

1.1 Clustering and co-clustering approaches to part-of-speech induction in language acquisition research

Single-mode clustering approaches

Clustering algorithms operate on a two-dimensional matrix where the rows and columns in this context represent words and the linguistic contexts in which they appear, taken from a corpus of natural language, and the cells of the matrix contain frequency counts of how often a word occurs in a particular context. It has often been proposed that children might make use of information about the contextual distribution of usage of words to induce the parts-of-speech of their native language (e.g. Maratsos & Chalkley, 1980), and work by, e.g., Redington, Chater & Finch (1998) and Clark (2000), showed that parts-of-speech can indeed be induced by clustering together words that are used in similar contexts in a corpus. Clustering word types together does not take into account the fact that the part-of-speech of a word type may change depending on the context in which it is used. One of the most influential models in part-of-speech induction in language acquisition, the Frequent Frames model of Mintz (2003), addresses this issue by forming clusters of the contextual frames in which words are used, rather than the words themselves. The idea is that the contexts define the part-of-speech, rather than the words themselves. This model attains high, but not perfect results in part-of-speech tagging for English child-directed speech; part of the reason is that even frames are sometimes ambiguous in the parts-of-speech that they can accommodate, and Erkelens (2008) has shown that this problem is more pronounced when the Frequent Frames approach is applied to Dutch material. In general, however the set of frame contexts is chosen, the problem of contextual ambiguity is likely to present itself. Hence, an approach is needed in which both words and contexts can be associated with multiple categories. Techniques of co-clustering, also called biclustering or two-mode clustering, (see Madeira & Oliveira, 2004, Van Mechelen et al., 2004, for reviews), represent one such approach.

Co-clustering approaches

Single-mode clustering forms clusters of elements in one dimension of the matrix (either rows or columns) by grouping together elements on the basis of similar co-occurrence with elements of the other dimension. Co-clustering techniques, on the other hand, form clusters on the basis of similarity between rows and similarity between columns simultaneously. Co-clustering is therefore able to assign row and column elements to the same clusters. We can distinguish between row-column clustering methods which assign each row and each column to a particular cluster, and data clustering methods which assign each individual non-empty cell of the matrix to a cluster. Some co-clustering methods allow for overlapping clusters, i.e. in row-column methods by allowing rows and columns to belong to more than one cluster, or in data clustering methods by allowing cells in the matrix to belong to more than one cluster. Co-clustering algorithms have been shown to be useful in many applications, notably in the analysis of gene expression data (Madeira & Oliveira, 2004).

There are good reasons to prefer a co-clustering approach over a single-mode categorization approach in part-of-speech induction. In natural language, including child-directed speech, there are many cases where a word appears in a context that does not specify the part-of-speech exactly, but allows several possibilities, while at the same time, the word is also ambiguous in its part-of-speech. Co-clustering is able to deal with part-of-speech ambiguity at the level of word and frame simultaneously. For example, a common frame in child-directed speech in English is "That's X.", where the word that fills the X slot could be a noun ("That's ice-cream.") or an adjective ("That's pretty."). Simultaneously, the word "mean" can be used as either a verb or an adjective (the nominal usage is rare in child-directed speech). A single-mode clustering algorithm that aims to assign a part-of-speech to the word "mean" in "That's mean" will be unable to decide between the allowed parts-of-speech for the frame, if frames were clustered, and between the allowed parts-of-speech for the words, if words were clustered. However, a co-clustering approach that assigned "That's X" to both the categories noun and adjective, and "mean" to the categories verb and adjective, would be able to deduce that the only category that the word and the frame have in common is adjective, and therefore that this is the correct category. In this way, co-clustering is better able to deal with linguistic ambiguity.

Even apart from its practical utility in part-of-speech induction, co-clustering is broadly compatible with a psychological outlook that conceives of part-of-speech development in terms of associative learning (see e.g. Shanks, 1995). Under this view, parts-of-speech are mental categories that are formed by repeated exposure to words used in context, in combination with whatever semantic construal the language-learning child places on the utterances she hears.

Only a few studies have applied co-clustering to part-of-speech induction with child-directed language (but see Freitag, 2004, for part-of-speech induction with co-clustering on adult-directed language in the Penn Treebank). The pioneering work in this regard was the EMILE system of Adriaans and colleagues (Adriaans, 1992), which formed co-clusters of word-context combinations as a step in the process of inducing rules for a categorial grammar. While the grammars formed in this way perform well, EMILE typically produces large, overlapping categories which do not correspond to the parts-of-speech of English (Adriaans, 1999). Hence, it is difficult to evaluate the accuracy of EMILE's part-of-speech tagging against a gold standard.

Leibbrandt & Powers (2008) applied co-clustering to a corpus of English child-directed speech, yielding accuracy comparable to that obtained by the Frequent Frames model of Mintz (2003). This approach was also able to outperform Frequent Frames in tagging child-directed data in Dutch (Leibbrandt & Powers, 2010).

In this paper, we extend the work of Leibbrandt & Powers (2008, 2010) by describing and evaluating a novel co-clustering technique for part-of-speech induction. In Section 2 we present the Conflict-Driven Co-Clustering algorithm, and in Section 3 we evaluate its performance in part-of-speech tagging of a corpus of child-directed speech. We show that the algorithm delivers performance comparable to that of both the Frequent Frames model of Mintz (2003) and the co-clustering work by Leibbrandt & Powers (2008, 2010), and is more robust than the earlier work in automatically discovering the main English open classes of noun, verb and adjective, discarding smaller and less-easily interpretable categories. In Section 4 we consider reasons for these results and point to future directions for this work.

2 Conflict-Driven Co-Clustering

The Conflict-Driven Co-Clustering (CDCC) algorithm is a row-column-based co-clustering algorithm. It creates an initial clustering of words into a set of clusters, and a simultaneous clustering of frames into the same set of clusters. Only a few word and frame types are clustered to start with, and hence this initial clustering is inadequate to account for the empirical co-occurrence data (as explained below). From this starting point, the CDCC algorithm iteratively adds frames and clusters to the clusters, until all of the co-occurrence data is accounted for.

We make the assumption that there exist a number of parts-of-speech in the target language, and that a particular word used in a particular frame context belongs to only one part-of-speech[1]. We also assume that the word type is a cue to the part-of-speech, and that the same is true of the frame type. Finally, each word type and frame type is presumed to have the potential to be associated with more than one part-of-speech.

Suppose, then, that we (in this case, the co-clustering algorithm, but also, potentially, a child learning the target language) already have some notion of the parts-of-speech to which a particular frame type *f* "belongs", and the parts-of-speech to which a word type *w* belongs. Then when we encounter an instance (i.e. a token) of the word type *w* used in the context of the frame type *f*, and wish to assign a part-of-speech to this instance, the only viable candidates (based on our knowledge at the time) are those parts-of-speech that both *w* and *f* have in common. Should there be multiple such candidates, a part-of-speech tagging algorithm might resort to combining information about the probabilities of *f* and *w* belonging to each candidate in order to select a "winner". However, when there is *no* such candidate (word and frame have no part-of-speech in common), this presents a problem for part-of-speech tagging. Such a situation is an instance of the "conflicts" from which CDCC derives its name.

More concretely, we can represent the cluster membership of each of the J words under consideration as a $J \times K$ matrix W, where K is the number of clusters, and $W_{jk} = 1$ if word j is a member of cluster k, and 0 otherwise. Similarly, the cluster membership of each of the I frames is represented by the $I \times K$ matrix F, where $F_{ik} = 1$ if frame i belongs to cluster k, and 0 otherwise.

The $I \times J$ matrix D represents the co-occurrence data obtained from the corpus, where $D_{ij} = 1$ if word j occurs in the context of frame i in the corpus, and 0 otherwise. Then a conflict exists whenever $D_{ij} = 1$ and the dot-product $W_j \cdot F_i = 0$.

We can think of the possibilities described by the cluster membership matrices W and F as accounting for the word-frame co-occurrences described in D: if a word and frame can occur together, there must be at least one part-of-speech to which they both belong. Conflicts occur where cells in the D matrix are not yet accounted for in this way. The problem to be solved in this case, therefore, is to remove all

[1] There are examples, even in the corpus used in this experiment, for which this assumption does not seem to hold; however, these examples are relatively infrequent enough to warrant its use as a useful heuristic.

instances of conflict. Because the *D* matrix is empirically given, the only way to remove conflict is to modify the *F* and *W* matrices so that all co-occurrences in *D* can be accounted for.

Figure 1 illustrates some cases of conflict and resolved conflict between word and frame. Initially, the utterance "Shall I brush it?" contains a conflict, because the frame "Shall I X it?" is allocated to the Verb category, but "brush" is not yet allocated to any category. The conflict might be resolved by adding "brush" to the Verb category. Later, when we consider the utterance "There's your brush", a conflict would occur if "brush" was allocated to Verb only and "There's your X" was allocated to Noun only. Suppose that the conflict was resolved correctly by also adding "brush" to the category Noun (in addition to already being allocated to Verb). Then when the utterance "Don't brush it" is encountered, there is no conflict, as both "Don't X it" and "brush" are allocated to the Verb cluster, and hence the allocations are compatible.

Shall I brush it?	N	V	A
brush	0	**0**	0
Shall I X it?	0	**1**	0

There's your brush.	N	V	A
brush	**0**	**1**	0
There's your X.	**1**	**0**	0

Don't brush it.	N	V	A
brush	1	1	0
Don't X it.	0	1	0

Figure 1. Three instances of conflict and non-conflict. In the top example, *brush* and *Shall I X it?* are in conflict, in the middle example, *brush* and *There's your X* are in conflict, and in the lower example there is no conflict. (N = Noun, V = Verb, A = Adjective)

An open problem is then how best to calculate the cluster membership matrices *W* and *F* so as to remove all conflicts. One obvious "solution" would be to simply add membership of every cluster to every word and frame. While this would remove all conflicts, it is clearly not a useful basis for part-of-speech tagging, and violates our sense that not every word or context can belong to every part-of-speech.

A better approach might be to start with a very sparse pair of initial matrices for *W* and *F*, which greatly under-determine the co-occurrence matrix *D*, and then add cluster memberships to individual frames and words (changing 0s to 1s in *F* and *W*) if adding them would help to solve conflicts.

We still need to decide which cluster memberships to add, and a useful principle might be to add memberships parsimoniously, i.e. to try to minimize the number of new memberships added to *F* and *W*. The CDCC algorithm takes a greedy approach to this problem. On each iteration, it simply adds the single cluster membership (word or frame) that would resolve the largest number of conflicts existing at that time. The set of remaining conflicts is then recalculated, and the cluster membership that again resolves the greatest number of conflicts is added, with the process being repeated until all conflicts have been resolved.

The only remaining point to specify is how the algorithm gets started, i.e. how the *W* and *F* matrices are initialized. It would be desirable to begin with just a small number of "ground truths", i.e. a small number of category memberships, for only a few frames and words, that are well-established in advance. The rest of the values in the membership matrices are then bootstrapped from this starting point by referring to the co-occurrence matrix.

The initial values with which *W* and *F* are "seeded" can come from any source: for instance, they may be the result of a process of semantic category formation (e.g. Macnamara, 1982; Pinker, 1984), so that words that refer to physical objects are flagged as belonging to one category, and words for actions marked as belonging to another category (bear in mind that this does not preclude these words from later also being assigned to other categories). This process might also be extended to frames that reliably contain words referring to objects, actions, physical properties, etc. In computational work on language acquisition, proxies for these categories might be obtained from lists of early-acquired words, possibly in combination with norms on word imageability. In less acquisition-oriented work, seeds may be obtained from manually annotated examples, so that this becomes a semi-supervised approach to part-of-speech tagging.

In the experiment reported here, we decided to obtain our seed information entirely from the same word-frame co-occurrence matrix *D* used later to expand the *W* and *F* matrices, and we did so along the same lines as followed by Leibbrandt & Powers (2008, 2010). Consequently, our results are prone to some of the shortcomings of the earlier work, as discussed later. We emphasize that the choice of seeding algorithm is not part of the CDCC algorithm proper, and informal experimentation has shown that the performance of CDCC is highly dependent on the accuracy of the initial seed information.

2.1 CDCC Algorithm

The conflict-driven co-clustering algorithm (pseudo-code is presented in Box 2) attempts to find a conflict-free allocation of categories to words and frames. It does so by repeatedly removing the largest existing conflict until no conflicts remain.

In what follows, we use the term "co-item" to refer to those items with which an item (word or frame) co-occurs in *D*, i.e. the co-items of a word type are the frame types in which it has occurred, and the co-items of a frame type are the word types that have occurred in it. Conflicts between items and their co-items are removed by simply allocating those additional categories to items that they would need in order to no longer be in conflict with the co-items. Conflicts are not resolved in random order; instead, the conflict resolution option that would resolve the largest number of conflicts is chosen at every step. In this way, the membership vectors for each of the words and frames are adjusted so as to converge onto the "correct" allocation. When no more changes can be made to the membership vectors, the algorithm halts.

The algorithm works in batch mode, considering the entire data matrix at once. For every item (whether word or frame), the set of co-items that are currently in conflict with the item is collected. Using the current membership matrices *W* and *F*, the algorithm allows each co-item to cast one vote for every category to which it is currently allocated (i.e. co-items cast votes to have particular categories added to the item's allocations). Per definition, these are categories that the target item does not have in its membership vector, so that adding that category to the item's membership vector would resolve the conflict between the item and that particular co-item; however, the point of voting is to find the single change that would result in the *largest number* of conflict resolutions at once. The number of votes for each category is determined in this way for every target item (every word and every frame). The suggested category allocation that has received the largest number of votes over all words and all frames is designated the "winner", and the category in question is added to the membership vector of the item in question.

<u>CDCC</u>:

D: co-occurrence matrix of frames and words

F, W: membership matrices describing the categories to which each of the frames and words may belong. F and W are initialized prior to running CDCC, for instance using unsupervised clustering as in Box 2. F[k][i] = 1 if frame i is able to belong to cluster k, and 0 otherwise, and similarly for W.

```
repeat until convergence (see text)
  for i = 1 to I
    for j = 1 to J
      if D[ i ][ j ] = 1
         conflict = true
         for k = 1 to K
            if (F [ k ][ i ] = 1
            and W [ k ][ j ] = 1)
               conflict =false
         if conflict
            tallyVotes(i, j)
  find k1 such that FrameVotes[ k1 ][ i ] =
      max cell in FrameVotes
  find k2 such that WordVotes[ k2 ][ j ] =
      max cell in WordVotes
  if FrameVotes[k1][ i ] > WordVotes[k2][ j ]
      F [ k1 ][ i ] = 1
  else
      W [ k2 ][ j ] = 1

tallyVotes(i, j):
  for k = 1 to K
    if (F[ k ][ i ] = 0 and W [ k ][ j ] = 1)
          FrameVotes[ k ][ i ] += 1
    else if (F [ k ][ i ] = 1 and W [ k ][ j ] = 0)
          WordVotes[ k ][ j ] += 1
```

Box 1. Conflict-Driven Co-Clustering Algorithm.

One of the benefits of the voting system is that it is self-correcting. If an item which is, say, a Noun, is incorrectly not assigned to the cluster corresponding to Nouns, then it will cast one incorrect vote each time to change the allocation of each of its co-items. However, the co-items are likely to be Nouns in most cases, and hence to occur in other Noun frames, which will in most cases lend them the Noun allocation, so that they will vote en masse to change the allocation of the incorrectly allocated item to Noun.

The product of the CDCC algorithm is a fairly conservative allocation of (potentially multiple) clusters to each of the words and frames.

3 Evaluation of the algorithms

The CDCC algorithm was applied to a corpus of child-directed speech, after which individual tokens of word-frame co-occurrences were categorized into one of the co-clusters produced by the algorithm, as described below.

3.1 Data Set

The data set used was the same as in Leibbrandt & Powers (2008), namely the child-directed portion of the Manchester corpus (Theakston, Lieven, Pine & Rowland, 2001) obtained from the CHILDES project (MacWhinney, 2000). This corpus is supplied with a manual part-of-speech tagging, which was used as the 'gold standard' correct tagging against which the categorization produced by CDCC was evaluated.

3.2 Extraction of Contextual Frames

Contextual frames were extracted from the corpus following the method in Leibbrandt & Powers (2008). Frames were formed from utterances in the corpus by replacing all but the most frequently-occurring words in the corpus with a placeholder symbol, turning corpus utterances into lexically-based schematic template sentences with slots that can be filled by inserting single words (for example, "Don't X it", "That's your X", "It's very X"). Frequency counts were collected of the number of occurrences of each word in each of the contextual frames, and the resulting data matrix was filtered to contain only those elements that attained a certain level of support, i.e. frames that occurred with 5 or more distinct word types, and words that occurred in 5 or more frame types. The resulting data matrix was used to obtain seed category membership information for selected words and frames, as described in the next section.

3.3 Seed Information

The first step in obtaining "ground truth" seed information for running the CDCC algorithm (pseudocode shown in Box 2) is to perform a

```
D: co-occurrence matrix, such that D [ i ][ j ] = 1
if word j has co-occurred with frame I, 0
otherwise.
Allocation: Cluster membership vector for
frames, obtained from hard clustering algorithm,
such that Allocation[ i ] = k if frame i is allocated
to cluster k.

Initialize ClusterCoocc[ K ][ J ] to all zeroes.
for i = 1 to I
  for j = 1 to J
    if D[ i ][ j ]
      ClusterCoocc [ Allocation[ i ] ] [ j ] += 1
for k = 1 to K
  sum = sum(ClusterCoocc [ k ])
  for j = 1 to J
    Distribution[ k ][ j ].index = j
    Distribution[ k ][ j ].value =
      ClusterCoocc [ k ][ j ] / sum
  Sort Distribution[ k ] by value (descending)
  cumulativeProportion = 0; j = 0
  repeat until cumulativeProportion ≥ η
    j += 1
    index = Distribution[ k ][ j ].index
    value = Distribution[ k ][ j ].value
    SeedWords[ k ] [index] = 1
    cumulativeProportion += value
for each pair (SeedWords[a], SeedWords[b]),
  a ≠ b
    Remove all words that occur in both
    SeedWords[a] and SeedWords[b]
for i = 1 to I
  for j = 1 to J
    if D [ i ][ j ]
      for k = 1 to K
        if SeedWords[ k ][ j ] = 1
          SeedFrames[ k ][ i ] = 1
for each pair (SeedFrames[a], SeedFrames[b]),
  a ≠ b
    Remove all frames that occur in both
    SeedFrames[a] and SeedFrames[b]
```

Box 2. Seed frame and word selection algorithm.

standard one-mode clustering of the (L2-normalized) frame vectors of the co-occurrence matrix *D*, producing clusters of contextual frames (hierarchical clustering with average linkage was used in this experiment).

Next, we select sets of words that are particularly distinctive of each of the frame clusters. The assumption is that words that occur in a large number of frame types from a particular cluster are good representatives of that cluster. Hence, for each cluster, words are ranked in order of the number of distinct frame types from the cluster in which each word has occurred, and are added one-by-one to the seed-word set for the cluster, until the cumulative proportion of total distinct-frame counts accounted for exceeds a threshold (set to 0.25 in this experiment). Once all seed-word sets have been collected in this way, seed-words which occur in the sets of more than one cluster are discarded.

Next, a seed-frame set is created for each cluster, consisting of all frames which occurred with seed-words from that cluster and did not occur with a seed-word from any other cluster. The resulting seed sets are arguably the words and frames that are the most distinctly associated with each cluster. The process described above can be considered to produce similar results to a psychological process of association between clusters and words, where the strength of association between the cluster and the word is strengthened each time the word is used in a frame that is strongly associated with that cluster already. Each distinct frame is considered to contribute an equal amount of activation strength to the word, regardless of its own frequency of occurrence in the input, so that this association process is sensitive to the type frequency of frames co-occurring with the word in question, rather than to the token frequency. A wider range of co-occurring frames constitutes more robust evidence that the word does indeed belong with the cluster (and most likely possesses many of the semantic attributes that are associated with the cluster). For evidence that the type frequency of words occurring in a frame aids generalization, see Bybee (1985, 2006).

The algorithm maintains a binary-valued allocation vector for each frame and each word of length K, where K is the number of clusters. The k'th value in the allocation vector is 1 if the word or frame can belong to cluster k, and 0 if not. In this way, the algorithms deal with the ambiguity of both words and frames, by allowing an item to belong to more than one cluster. For every cluster k, the k'th value of the allocation vector of every seed word and every seed frame of cluster k is initialized to 1, and all other values are set to 0.

3.4 Categorization

For the purpose of evaluation, we categorize each of the instances of word-frame co-occurrences in the data matrix D by combining the word and frame cluster information contained in the membership matrices W and F. When classifying a particular instance of word w used in frame f, if there exists a unique a cluster c such that w and f have both been allocated to c (in a majority of cases in this experiment, there was such a unique cluster), then the word-frame combination is classified as belonging to the cluster in question. In cases where the word and frame have more than one cluster in common, we fall back on estimating the amount of evidence that the word and frame separately belong to each of the clusters. The fallback values for each word and frame are calculated as the proportion of co-items of the word or frame that are allocated to each cluster. The fallback value of the word is multiplied by the fallback value of the frame, for each cluster separately, and the cluster with the highest product is selected as the category to which the frame-word combination is assigned.

3.5 Evaluation Measures

Results are reported in terms of standard measures of precision, recall and F-score, with random baselines in parentheses. These measures were calculated, as is customary in unsupervised categorization, by a pair counting approach that constructs a confusion matrix based on whether *pairs of elements* are assigned to the same category in the gold-standard, and also in the clustering model (see e.g. Mintz, Newport & Bever, 2002). Because of several well-known shortcomings of precision and recall (e.g. Powers, 2003; Rosenberg & Hirschberg, 2007), we also report the Informedness measure (Powers, 2003), which corresponds to the probability that the predictions made by the algorithm are informed, in the sense of making correct use of information.

For a 2×2 contingency table with the symbols a, b, c and d respectively indicating the number of true positives, false positives, false negatives and true negatives, Informedness is given by

$$I = \frac{a}{a+c} - \frac{b}{b+d}.$$

Informedness can thus be expressed as Recall for a particular cluster, discounted by the proportion of all non-category items that occur in that cluster. Informedness is equivalent to the well-known delta-P formula expressing association strength in human associative learning (e.g. Shanks, 1995). For a supervised classification problem, with a table of arbitrary dimensions $m \times m$, Informedness is calculated for the 2×2 contingency table of each category in turn, and the Informedness values for all categories are combined in a weighted sum, where the weight for each category is the proportion of word tokens assigned to that category by the algorithm (i.e. the algorithm's bias to assign instances to the category). In unsupervised cases, it is not obvious how to associate clusters with gold-standard categories. In this case, weighted Informedness values are calculated for every possible 1-to-1 mapping between gold standard categories and clusters, and the highest of these Informedness values is selected.

For evaluation, we made use of only those tokens that were assigned to one of the three major open-class categories (nouns, verbs and adjectives).

	HC	CDCC	LP08	FreqF
Precision	0.844 *(0.559)*	0.888 *(0.559)*	0.900 *(0.559)*	0.90
Recall	0.774 *(0.513)*	0.911 *(0.574)*	0.886 *(0.551)*	0.91
F	0.808 *(0.535)*	0.899 *(0.566)*	0.893 *(0.555)*	0.90
I	0.708	0.800	0.814	n/a

Table 1. Performance of clustering-based part-of-speech induction methods. Random baseline values in italics. Baseline value for Informedness is zero. *HC* = Hierarchical Clustering (one-dimensional); *CDCC* = Conflict-Driven Co-Clustering; *LP08* = replication of Leibbrandt & Powers (2008); *FreqF* = Frequent Frames (results from Mintz, 2006, baseline and Informedness scores unknown).

3.6 Results

The results of categorization according to the *CDCC* algorithm is shown in Table 1. For comparison, we have also shown the results of categorization with three other algorithms, namely: *LP08*, a replication of Leibbrandt & Powers (2008); *FreqF*, the results from Mintz (2003) for the Frequent Frames model applied to the same corpus as used here; and *HC*, the results from categorizing a word-frame combination according to the cluster of the frame only, where the frame clusters are the ones derived in the one-way clustering step that produced the seed information for CDCC.

The results show that CDCC is competitive in its categorization performance with both the LP08 and FreqF approaches. Comparing Informedness and F-scores against their random baselines, the performance of LP08 is only slightly better than that of the two new algorithms (random baseline values were not reported by Mintz, 2003). Importantly, CDCC (as well as LP08) performs much better than the hard clustering HC from which it derives its seed information, showing that co-clustering improves categorization.

3.7 Robustness of induced parts-of-speech

We have not yet said much about the number of clusters formed by the co-clustering algorithms. This number could conceivably be influenced by the number of clusters formed by the initial one-way clustering algorithm, which is often (as it was in our experiment) a parameter under control of the experimenter. However, the number of parts-of-speech produced by a part-of-speech induction algorithm should be relatively immune to manipulations of algorithmic parameters. A related issue is that the parts-of-speech produced by clustering approaches are often unsatisfactory from a linguistic point of view, as they don't correspond exactly to the expected parts-of-speech of the target language (see also Schütze, 1995). We regard it as desirable for a part-of-speech induction method to account for at least the main open-class parts-of-speech of English (nouns, verbs, adjectives and adverbs), and to be able to produce these without undue coercion.

Therefore, it is of interest to consider how the number of parts-of-speech produced by the co-clustering algorithms is affected by the number of clusters in the original one-way clustering from which they start. These results are shown in Table 2. The table shows the number of parts-of-speech produced by LP08 versus CDCC when started off with varying numbers of hard clusters in the range 3 to 18. For each algorithm, the table shows (under *Any*) the number of distinct parts-of-speech (clusters) to which at least one word-frame occurrence was assigned during the categorization reported above, and also (under *1%*) the number of parts-of-speech such that at least one percent of the total number of word-frame combinations were assigned to that part-of-speech. The results under *Any* show that, as

	LP08		CDCC	
K	Any	1%	Any	1%
3	3	3	3	3
6	5	3	4	3
9	9	4	5	3
12	12	6	9	3
15	15	6	10	3
18	18	7	9	3

Table 2. Number of parts-of-speech used during categorization for three co-clustering algorithms, for varying *K* = number of clusters produced in initial one-way clustering. *Any* = number of parts-of-speech that account for at least one frame-word instance; *1%* = number of parts-of-speech that account for at least 1% of instances. *LP08* = replication of Leibbrandt & Powers (2008); *CDCC* = Conflict-Driven Co-Clustering.

the number of initial clusters grew, so too did the number of clusters that were used at least once during categorization, so that the algorithms were rather badly prone to proliferation of parts-of-speech when started with a large number of initial clusters, although CDCC was more conservative than LP08, and managed to discard many of the original clusters. However, the results for *1%* are more encouraging. Both algorithms, even when started with several candidate clusters in the one-way clustering, managed to eliminate the minor clusters to some extent, and redistribute their members into the larger parts-of-speech. It is particularly noteworthy that for CDCC, only three clusters were used for more than 1% of all instances. Inspection of the details of categorization showed that the CDCC algorithm managed to discover three clusters that seemed to correspond closely to the three major English parts-of-speech of Noun, Verb and Adjective. These categories appeared to be such a salient feature of the data for CDCC that they were able to 'self-organize' during runs of the algorithm from various one-way clustering starting points. This robust induction of the main English parts-of-speech is a striking advantage of CDCC over LP08.

It may be argued that the number of classes produced by the algorithm are too few to provide a basis for part-of-speech induction. To some extent this is a consequence of the seeding algorithm chosen. The frames used by Leibbrandt & Powers (2008, 2010) tended to support mostly open-class word fillers; nouns, verbs and adjectives made up respectively 52%, 25% and 10% of the total number of tokens that served as fillers in their frames, for a total of 87%. Arguably, this may be seen as desirable: for a child learning a language, knowledge of the open classes is more useful for learning novel words than knowledge of the closed classes. On the other hand, the lack of a category of adverbs may be regarded as a shortcoming of the original work by Leibbrandt & Powers. Nevertheless, the CDCC algorithm was able to robustly identify the main classes represented in the co-occurrence matrix.

4 Discussion

The CDCC algorithm has been shown to achieve similar categorization performance to some earlier models of part-of-speech induction. The most striking advantage has been that CDCC is able to "hone in" on the three main parts-of-speech. We suggest that this is due to the conservative nature of conflict resolution: by tallying the strength of evidence for a particular category in terms of the number of votes it receives, weaker categories are not able to cast sufficient numbers of votes to change word or frame allocations. Importantly, this means that in subsequent iterations, when conflicts are recalculated and votes cast once more, allocations of particular words or frames to these minor categories are more likely to be swamped by the additional allocations previously added to the major categories, so that the initially stronger categories become stronger as the algorithm executes while the weaker categories all but disappear. This is an important feature of the algorithm, because the original clustering step from which both CDCC and Leibbrandt & Powers (2008) begin is unconstrained in the number of clusters it produces; this is a parameter of the system, but it is a relatively unimportant one in the case of CDCC because the algorithm self-organizes around the major categories.

While the CDCC algorithm performs similarly to other established work while taking a radically different approach, several issues remain to be investigated. One of the potential strengths of CDCC is that it treats category membership in a discrete or symbolic way, rather than graded, as in Leibbrandt & Powers (2008). It remains to be seen whether such a treatment provides specific benefits in resolving ambiguity when dealing with words or frames that can belong to multiple categories.

CDCC has been formulated here as combining distributional information about the word type and the frame type in order to produce a part-of-speech allocation. However, the algorithm can be viewed more generally as a method to combine or fuse more than one source of information together, and hence can be applied to distributional, phonological, semantic or any other forms of linguistic information.

As it has been formulated here as a batch process, the CDCC algorithm can be regarded as addressing only the computational level of the problem of part-of-speech induction in language acquisition. Additional work would be required to attempt to address the algorithmic or implementational levels by turning the algorithm into a fully incremental learner (e.g., Parisien, Fazly & Stevenson, 2008; Chrupala & Alishahi, 2010). A simple variant of the CDCC algorithm could be one that simply processes the corpus in order, and in the case of a conflict between word and frame, stores the occurrence as evidence that the membership of either the word or frame should be altered, and in what way. When the accumulated evidence for a specific change of membership exceeds a threshold (e.g. when a certain number of votes have been cast to add membership of a particular cluster to a word or frame), the membership is added. It would remain to be determined empirically whether this iterative variant is still able to exhibit the same categorization performance and the property of robustness shown above for the batch CDCC algorithm.

References

Adriaans, P. (1992). *Language Learning from a Categorial Perspective.* Unpublished PhD thesis, University of Amsterdam.

Adriaans, P. (1999). *Learning Shallow Context-Free Languages under Simple Distributions* (Technical Report No. PP-1999-13): Institute for Logic, Language and Computation, University of Amsterdam.

Berg-Kirkpatrick, T., Côté, A.B., DeNero, J. & Klein, D. (2010). Painless unsupervised learning with features. *Proceedings of NAACL 2010*, 582–590.

Bybee, J. L. (1985). *Morphology: a study of the relation between meaning and form*: John Benjamins.

Bybee J. L. (2006). From usage to grammar: the mind's response to repetition. *Language, 82*,711–733.

Christodoulopoulos, C., Goldwater, S. & Steedman, M. (2010). Two Decades of Unsupervised POS induction: How far have we come? *Proceedings of EMNLP 2010*, 575-584.

Chrupala, G. & Alishahi, A. (2010). Online Entropy-based Model of Lexical Category Acquisition. *Proceedings of the 14th Conference on Computational Natural Language Learning (CoNLL-2010).*

Clark, A. (2000). Inducing syntactic categories by context distribution clustering. *Proceedings of the Conference on Natural Language Learning (CONLL-2000),* 91–94.

Erkelens, M. (2008). Restrictions of frequent frames as cues to categories: the case of Dutch. *Supplement to the Proceedings of the 32nd Boston University Conference on Language Development (BUCLD 32).*

Freitag, D. (2004). Toward unsupervised whole-corpus tagging. *Proceedings of COLING-04*, 357-363.

Goldwater, S. & Griffiths, T. (2007). A fully Bayesian approach to unsupervised part-of-speech tagging. *Proceedings of ACL 2007*, 744–751,

Leibbrandt, R. E., & Powers, D. M. W. (2008). Grammatical category induction using lexically-based templates. *Supplement to the Proceedings of the 32nd Boston University Conference on Language Development (BUCLD 32).*

Leibbrandt, R.E. & Powers, D.M. (2010). Frequent Frames as Cues to Part-of-Speech in Dutch: Why Filler Frequency Matters. *Proceedings of the 32nd Annual Conference of the Cognitive Science Society*, 2680-2685.

MacWhinney, B. (2000). *The CHILDES Project: Tools for analyzing talk.* (3rd ed. Vol. 2: The database). Mahwah, NJ: Lawrence Erlbaum.

Macnamara, J. (1982). *Names for things: a study of child language*. Cambridge, MA: MIT Press.

Madeira, S. C., & Oliveira, A. L. (2004). Biclustering algorithms for biological data analysis: A survey. *IEEE Transactions on Computational Biology and Bioinformatics, 1*(1), 24-45.

Maratsos, M. P., & Chalkley, M. A. (1980). The internal language of children's syntax: The ontogenesis and representation of syntactic categories. In K. E. Nelson (Ed.), *Children's Language* (Vol. 2). New York: Gardner Press.

Mintz, T. H. (2003). Frequent frames as a cue for grammatical categories in child directed speech. *Cognition, 90*(1), 91-117.

Mintz, T. H., Newport, E. L., & Bever, T. G. (2002). The distributional structure of grammatical categories in speech to young children. *Cognitive Science, 26*, 393-424.

Moon, T., Erk, K. & Baldridge, J. (2010) Crouching Dirichlet, Hidden Markov Model: Unsupervised POS Tagging with Context Local Tag Generation. *Proceedings of EMNLP 2010*, 196-206.

Parisien, C., Fazly, A. & Stevenson, S. (2008). An incremental Bayesian model for learning syntactic categories. *Proceedings of the 12th Conference on Computational Natural Language Learning, (CONLL-2008).*

Pinker, S. (1984). *Language learnability and language development*. Cambridge, MA: Harvard University Press.

Powers, D. M. W. (2003). *Recall and precision versus the Bookmaker*. Paper presented at the 4th International Conference on Cognitive Science (ICCS).

Redington, M., Chater, N., & Finch, S. (1998). Distributional information: A powerful cue for acquiring syntactic categories. *Cognitive Science, 22*(4), 425-469.

Rosenberg, A. & Hirschberg, J. (2007). V-Measure: A Conditional Entropy-Based External Cluster Evaluation Measure. *Proceedings of the 2007 Joint Conference on Empirical Methods in Natural Language Processing and Computational Natural Language Learning (EMNLP-CoNLL-2007)*, pp. 410-420.

Schütze, H. (1995) Distributional part-of-speech tagging. *Proceedings of EACL-95.*

Shanks, D.R. (1995). *The psychology of associative learning*. Cambridge University Press.

St. Clair, M.C., Monaghan, P. & Christiansen, M. H. (2010). Learning grammatical categories from distributional cues: Flexible frames for language acquisition. *Cognition, 116*, 341-360.

Theakston, A. L., Lieven, E., Pine, J. M., & Rowland, C. F. (2001). The role of performance limitations in the acquisition of verb-argument structure: an alternative account. *Journal of Child Language, 28*, 127-152.

Van Mechelen, I. & De Boeck, P. (2004). Two-mode clustering methods: a structured overview. *Statistical Methods in Medical Research*, *13*, 363-394.

Dependency Parsing domain adaptation using transductive SVM

Antonio Valerio Miceli-Barone
University of Pisa, Italy /
Largo B. Pontecorvo, 3, Pisa, Italy
miceli@di.unipi.it

Giuseppe Attardi
University of Pisa, Italy /
Largo B. Pontecorvo, 3, Pisa, Italy
attardi@di.unipi.it

Abstract

Dependency Parsing domain adaptation involves adapting a dependency parser, trained on an annotated corpus from a given domain (e.g., newspaper articles), to work on a different target domain (e.g., legal documents), given only an unannotated corpus from the target domain.
We present a shift/reduce dependency parser that can handle unlabeled sentences in its training set using a transductive SVM as its action selection classifier.
We illustrate the the experiments we performed with this parser on a domain adaptation task for the Italian language.

1 Introduction

Dependency parsing is the task of identifying syntactic relationships between words of a sentence and labeling them according to their type. Typically, the dependency relationships are not defined by an explicit grammar, rather implicitly through a human-annotated corpus which is then processed by a machine learning procedure, yielding a parser trained on that corpus.
Shift-reduce parsers (Yamada and Matsumoto, 2003; Nivre and Scholz, 2004; Attardi, 2006) are an accurate and efficient (linear complexity) approach to this task: They scan the words of a sentence while updating an internal state by means of shift-reduce actions selected by a classifier trained on the annotated corpus.
Since the training corpora are made by human annotators, they are expensive to produce and are typically only available for few domains that don't adequately cover the whole spectrum of the language. Parsers typically lose significant accuracy when applied on text from domains not covered by their training corpus. Several techniques have been proposed to adapt a parser to a new domain, even when only unannotated samples from it are available (Attardi et al., 2007a; Sagae and Tsujii, 2007).
In this work we present a domain adaptation based on the semi-supervised training of the classifier of a shift-reduce parser. We implement the classifier as a multi-class SVM and train it with a transductive SVM algorithm that handles both labeled examples (generated from the source-domain annotated corpus) and unlabeled examples (generated from the the target-domain unannotated corpus).

2 Background

2.1 Shift-Reduce Parsing

A shift-reduce dependency parser is essentially a pushdown automaton that scans the sentence one token at a time in a fixed direction, while updating a stack of tokens and also updating a set of directed, labeled edges that is eventually returned as the dependency parse graph of the sentence.
Let T be the set of input token instances of the sentence and D be the set of dependency labels. The state of the parser is defined by the tuple $\langle s, q, p\rangle$, where $s \in T^*$ is the stack, $q \in T^*$ is the current token sequence and $p \in \{E | E \subseteq 2^{T\times T\times D}, E \text{ is a forest}\}$ is the current parse graph.
The parser starts in the state $\langle [], q_0, \{\}\rangle$, where q_0 is the input sentence, and terminates whenever it reaches a state in the form $\langle s, [], p\rangle$. At each step,

it performs one of the following actions:

$$\texttt{shift} : \frac{\langle s, [t|q], p\rangle}{\langle [t|s], q, p\rangle}$$

$$\texttt{rightreduce}_\texttt{d} : \frac{\langle [u|s], [t|q], p\rangle}{\langle s, [t|q], p \cup \{(u, t, d)\}\rangle}$$

$$\texttt{leftreduce}_\texttt{d} : \frac{\langle [u|s], [t|q], p\rangle}{\langle s, [u|q], p \cup \{(t, u, d)\}\rangle}$$

note that there are $rightreduce_d$ and $leftreduce_d$ actions for each label $d \in D$.

Action selection is done by the combination of two functions $f \circ c$: a feature extraction function $f : States \to \mathbb{R}^n$ that computes a (typically sparse) vector of numeric features of the current state and the multi-class classifier $c : \mathbb{R} \to Actions$. Alternatively, the classifier could score each available action, allowing a search procedure such as best-first (Sagae and Tsujii, 2007) or beam search to be used.

In our experiments we used an extension of this approach that has an additional stack and additional actions to handle non-projective dependency relationships (Attardi, 2006). Training is performed by computing, for each sentence in the annotated training corpus, a sequence of states and actions that generates its correct parse, yielding, for each transition, a training example $(x, y) \in \mathbb{R}^n \times Actions$ for the classifier.

Various classification algorithms have been successfully used, including maximum entropy, multi-layer perceptron, averaged perceptron, SVM, etc. In our approach, the classifier is always a multi-class SVM composed of multiple (one-per-parsing-action) two-class SVMs in one-versus-all configuration.

2.2 Parse Graph Revision

Attardi and Ciaramita (2007b) developed a method for improving parsing accuracy using parse graph revision: the output of the parser is fed to a procedure that scans the parsed sentence in a fixed direction and, at each step, possibly revises the current node (rerouting or relabeling its unique outgoing edge) based on the classifier's output.

Training is performed by parsing the training corpus and comparing the outcome against the annotation: for each sentence, a sequence of actions necessary to transform the machine-generated parse into the reference parse is computed and it is used to train the classifier. (Usually, a lower-quality parser is used during training, assuming that it will generate more errors and hence more revision opportunities).

This method tends to produce robust parsers: errors in the first stage have the opportunity to be corrected in the revision stage, thus, even if it does not learn from unlabeled data, it nevertheless performs well in domain adaptation tasks (Attardi et al., 2007a). In our experiments we used parse graph revision both as a baseline for accuracy comparison, and in conjunction with our approach (using a transductive SVM classifier in the revision stage).

2.3 Transductive SVM

Transductive SVM (Vapnik, 1998) is a framework for the semi-supervised training of SVM classifiers.

Consider the inductive (completely supervised) two-class SVM training problem: given a training set $\{(x_i, y_i)\,|x_i \in \mathbb{R}^n, y_i \in \{-1, 1\}\}_{i=1}^{L}$, find the maximum margin separation hypersurface $w \cdot \phi(x) + b = 0$ by solving the following optimization problem:

$$\arg\min_{w,\, b,\, \xi} \frac{1}{2}\|w\|_2^2 + C\sum_{i=1}^{L}\xi_i \qquad (1)$$

$$\begin{aligned} \forall i &: y_i\, w \cdot \phi(x) + b \geq 1 - \xi_i \\ \forall i &: \xi_i \geq 0 \\ & \quad w \in \mathbb{R}^m,\, b \in \mathbb{R} \end{aligned}$$

where $C \geq 0$ is a regularization parameter and $\phi(\cdot)$ is defined such that $k(x, \hat{x}) \equiv \phi(x) \cdot \phi(\hat{x})$ is the SVM kernel function. This is a convex quadratic programming problem that can be solved efficiently by specialized algorithms.

Including an unlabeled example set $\left\{x_j^*|x_j^* \in \mathbb{R}^n\right\}_{j=1}^{L^*}$ we obtain the transductive SVM training problem:

$$\arg\min_{w,\, b,\, \xi,\, y^*,\, xi^*} \frac{1}{2}\|w\|_2^2 + C\sum_{i=1}^{L}\xi_i + C^*\sum_{j=1}^{L^*}\xi_j^* \qquad (2)$$

$$
\begin{aligned}
\forall i &: y_i w \cdot \phi(x_i) + b \geq 1 - \xi_i \\
\forall j &: y_j^* w \cdot \phi(x_j^*) + b \geq 1 - \xi_j^* \\
\forall i &: \xi_i \geq 0 \\
\forall j &: \xi_j^* \geq 0 \\
\forall j &: y_j^* \in \{-1, 1\} \\
& \quad w \in \mathbb{R}^m, b \in \mathbb{R}
\end{aligned}
$$

This formulation essentially models the unlabeled examples the same way the labeled examples are modeled, with the key difference that the y_j^* (the unknown labels of the unlabeled examples) are optimization variables rather than parameters. Optimizing over these discrete variables makes the problem non-convex and in fact NP-hard. Nevertheless, algorithms that feasibly find a local minimum that is typically good enough for practical purposes do exist. In our experiments we used the iterative transductive SVM algorithm implemented in the SvmLight library (Joachims, 1999). This algorithm tends to become impractical when the number of unlabeled examples is greater than a few thousands, hence we were forced to use only a small portion on the available target domain corpus. We also tried the concave-convex procedure (CCCP) TSVM algorithm (Collobert et al., 2006) as implemented by the the Universvm package, and the multi-switch and deterministic annealing algorithms for linear TSVM (Sindhwani and Keerthi, 2007) as implemented by the Svmlin package. These methods are considerably faster but appear to be substantially less accurate than SvmLight on our training data.

3 Proposed approach

We present a semi-supervised training procedure for shift/reduce SVM parsers that allows to include unannotated sentences in the training corpus.

We randomly sample a small number (approx. 100) of sentences from the unannotated corpus (the target domain corpus in a domain adaptation task). For each of these sentences, we generate a sequence of states that the parser may encounter while scanning the sentence. For each state we extract the features to generate an unlabeled training example for the SVM classifier which is included in the training set along with the labeled examples generated from the annotated corpus. There is a caveat here: the parser state at any given point during the parsing of a sentence generally depends on the actions taken before, but when we are training on an unannotated sentence, we have no way of knowing what actions the parser should have taken, and thus the state we generate can be generally incorrect. For this reason we evaluated pre-parsing the unannotated sentences with a non-transductively trained parser in order to generate plausible state transitions while still adding unlabeled examples. However, it turned out that this pre-parsing does not seem to improve accuracy. We conjecture that, because the classifier does not see actual states but only features derived from them, and many of these features are independent of previous states and actions (features such as the lemma and POS tag of the current token and its neighbors have this property), these features contain enough information to perform parsing.

The classifier is trained using the SvmLight transductive algorithm. Since SvmLight supports only two-class SVMs while our classifier is multi-class (one class for each possible parsing action), we implement it in terms of two-class classifiers. We chose the one-versus-all strategy:

We train a number of sub-classifiers equal to the number of original classes. Each labeled training example (x, y) is converted to the example $(x, 1)$ for the sub-classifier number y and to the example $(x, -1)$ for the rest of sub-classifiers. Unlabeled examples are just replicated to all sub-classifiers. During classification the input example is evaluated by all the sub-classifiers and the one returning the maximum SVM score determines the class.

Our approach has been also applied to the second stage of the revision parser, by presenting the features of the unannotated sentences to the revision classifier as unlabeled training examples.

4 Experiments

4.1 Experimental setup

We performed our experiments using the DeSR parser (Attardi, 2006) on the data sets for the Evalita 2011 dependency parsing domain adaptation task for the Italian language (Evalita, 2011). The data set consists in an annotated source-domain corpus (newspaper articles) and an unannotated target-domain corpus (legal documents), plus a small annotated development corpus also from the target domain, which we used to evaluate the performance.

We performed a number of runs of the DeSR parser in various configurations, which differed in the number and type of features extracted, the sentence scanning direction, and whether or not parse tree revision was enabled. The SVM classifiers always used a quadratic kernel. In order to keep the running time of transductive SVM training acceptable, we limited the number of unannotated sentences to one hundred, which resulted in about 3200 unlabeled training examples fed to the classifiers. The annotated sentences were 3275.

We performed one run with 500 unannotated sentences and, at the cost of a greatly increased running time, the accuracy improvement was about 1%. We conjecture that a faster semi-supervised training algorithm could allow greater performance improvements by increasing the size of the unannotated corpus that can be processed. All the experiments were performed on a machine equipped with an quad-core Intel Xeon X3440 processor (8M Cache, 2.53 GHz) and 12 Gigabytes of RAM.

4.2 Discussion

As it is evidenced from the table in figure 1, our approach typically outperforms the non-transductive parser by about 1% of all the three score measures we considered. While the improvement is small, it is consistent with different configurations of the parser that don't use parse tree revision. Accuracy remained essentially equal or became slightly worse in the two configurations that use parse tree revision. This is possibly due to the fact that the first stage parser of the revision configurations uses a maximum entropy classifier during training that does not learn from the unlabeled examples.

These results suggest that unlabeled examples contain information that can exploited to improve the parser accuracy on a domain different than the labeled set domain. However, the computational cost of transductive learning algorithm we used limits the amount of unlabeled data we can exploit.

This is consistent with the results obtained by the self-training approaches, where a first parser is trained on a the labeled set, which is used to parse the unlabeled set which is then included into the training set of a second parser. (In fact, self-training is performed in the first step of the SvmLight TSVM algorithm).

Despite earlier negative results, (Sagae, 2010) showed that even naive self-training can provide accuracy benefits (about 2%) in domain adaptation, although these results are not directly comparable to ours because they refer to constituency parsing rather than dependency parsing. (McClosky et al., 2006) obtain even better results (5% f-score gain) using a more sophisticated form of self-training, involving n-best generative parsing and discriminative reranking. (Sagae and Tsujii, 2007) obtain similar gains (about 3 %) for dependency parsing domain adaptation, using self-training on a subset of the target-domain instances selected on the basis of agreement between two different parsers. (the results are not directly comparable to ours because they were obtained on a different corpus in a different language).

5 Conclusions and future work

We presented a semi-supervised training approach for shift/reduce SVM parsers and we illustrated an application to domain adaptation, with small but mostly consistent accuracy gains. While these gains may not be worthy enough to justify the extra computational cost of the transductive SVM algorithm (at least in the SvmLight implementation), they do point out that there exist a significant amount of information in an unannotated corpus that can be exploited for increasing parser accuracy and performing domain adaptation. We plan to further investigate this method by exploring classifier algorithms other than transductive SVM and combinations with other semi-supervised parsing approaches. We also plan to test our method on standardized English-language corpora to obtain results that are directly comparable to those in the literature.

References

H. Yamada and Y. Matsumoto. 2003. *Statistical Dependency Analysis with Support Vector Machines*. Proceedings of the 9th International Workshop on Parsing Technologies.

J. Nivre and M. Scholz. 2004. *Deterministic Dependency Parsing of English Text*. Proceedings of COLING 2004.

G. Attardi. 2006. *Experiments with a Multilanguage*

Figure 1: Experimental results

Accuracy (-R: right-to-left, -rev: left-to-right with revision, -rev2: right-to-left with revision):

	Transductive			Normal		
Parser configuration	LAS	UAS	Label only	LAS	UAS	Label only
6	**74.3**	**77.0**	**87.5**	73.1	75.5	86.7
6-R	**75.7**	**78.6**	**88.7**	74.6	77.6	87.8
6-rev	**75.2**	**78.2**	**88.6**	75.1	78.0	88.3
6-rev2	75.0	77.8	88.7	**75.8**	**78.6**	88.7
8	**74.3**	**77.0**	**87.3**	73.4	76.0	85.9
8-R	**75.7**	**78.6**	**88.7**	75.3	78.3	88.1
2	**74.7**	**77.4**	**87.4**	73.1	75.8	86.5

Figure 2: Typical features (configuration 6).

Numbers denote offsets.

'FEATS' denotes rich morphological features (grammatical number, gender, etc).

LEMMA	-2 -1 0 1 2 3 prev(0) leftChild(-1) leftChild(0) rightChild(-1) rightChild(0)
POSTAG	-2 -1 0 1 2 3 next(-1) leftChild(-1) leftChild(0) rightChild(-1) rightChild(0)
CPOSTAG	-1 0 1
FEATS	-1 0 1
DEPREL	leftChild(-1) leftChild(0) rightChild(-1)

Non-Projective Dependency Parser. Proceedings of CoNNL-X 2006.

G. Attardi, A. Chanev, M. Ciaramita, F. Dell'Orletta and M. Simi. 2007. *Multilingual Dependency Parsing and domain adaptation using DeSR*. Proceedings the CoNLL Shared Task Session of EMNLP-CoNLL 2007, Prague, 2007.

Kenji Sagae and Jun'ichi Tsujii. 2007. *Dependency parsing and domain adaptation with LR models and parser ensembles*. CoNLL Shared Task.

G. Attardi, M. Ciaramita. 2007. *Tree Revision Learning for Dependency Parsing*. Proc. of the Human Language Technology Conference 2007.

V. Vapnik. 1998. *Statistical Learning Theory*. Wiley.

Ronan Collobert and Fabian Sinz and Jason Weston and Lon Bottou and Thorsten Joachims. 2006. *Large Scale Transductive SVMs*. Journal of Machine Learning Research

Thorsten Joachims. 1999. *Transductive Inference for Text Classification using Support Vector Machines*. International Conference on Machine Learning (ICML), 1999.

Vikas Sindhwani and S. Sathiya Keerthi 2007. *Newton Methods for Fast Solution of Semisupervised Linear SVMs*. Large Scale Kernel Machines. MIT Press (Book Chapter), 2007

Kenji Sagae 2010. *Self-Training without Reranking for Parser Domain Adaptation and Its Impact on Semantic Role Labeling*. Proceedings of the 2010 Workshop on Domain Adaptation for Natural Language Processing. Uppsala, Sweden: Association for Computational Linguistics. p. 37-44

David McClosky, Eugene Charniak and Mark Johnson 2006. *Reranking and self-training for parser adaptation*. Proceeding ACL-44. Proceedings of the 21st International Conference on Computational Linguistics and the 44th annual meeting of the Association for Computational Linguistics

Evalita. 2011. *Domain Adaptation for Dependency Parsing*. .

Author Index